There Was a River

There Was a River

Bruce Berger

THE UNIVERSITY OF ARIZONA PRESS

Tucson and London

"Introduction," "The Light Brigade," "Blue," "The Face in the Canyon Wall," "A Cactus of Our Times," "Transition Zone," and parts of "Optic Nerve" were first published in *American Way*. A shorter version of "Comfort That Does Not Comprehend" first appeared in *Orion*.

The University of Arizona Press
Copyright © 1994
Arizona Board of Regents
All Rights Reserved
♾ This book is printed on acid-free, archival-quality paper.
Manufactured in the United States of America.

99 98 97 96 95 94   6 5 4 3 2 1

Library of Congress Cataloging-in-Publication Data
Berger, Bruce.
There was a river / Bruce Berger.
p.   cm.
ISBN 0-8165-1469-0 (acid-free paper). —
ISBN 0-8165-1493-3 (pb : acid-free paper)
1. Southwest, New—Description and travel.   2. Glen Canyon (Utah and Ariz.)   3. Berger, Bruce—Journeys—Glen Canyon (Utah and Ariz.)   I. Title.
F788.B47 1994   94-16296
979'.033'092—dc20   CIP

British Library Cataloguing-in-Publication Data
A catalogue record for this book is available from the British Library.

Contents

Introduction

A friend in New York, concerned about my lack of publishing contacts, took me on a tour of the island, climaxed by an appointment with the head of a major literary agency. We waited for a quarter of an hour in a room whose walls were covered solid with framed dust jackets. The outfit represented top novelists, political heavyweights, sports stars, the most fracturing humorists—all, it suddenly seemed, that was worth publishing. My heart pounded as a secretary summoned us down a long hall, then another hall, lined floor to ceiling with framed jackets too quickly and closely passed to identify, and to our audience with the great man. His desk was angled between windows at the corner of the building, with one view down an East Side avenue and another down a mid-town street. He was elegantly tailored, genial, shook our hands, and asked us to sit down. My friend had warned me of the man's passion for Ivy League sports, and I sat smiling vaguely while the two of them discussed the pigskin merits of Dartmouth,

Princeton, Harvard and the rest. At last the agent of agents turned to me and drawled, "You're a writer?"

"Yes," I said. "I've just published a nonfiction collection about the American deserts."

My friend, catching a raptor's shadow over the great man's face, rushed to mention a prize, certain reviews, but it was too late.

"About every five years," said this man who might make my future, folding his hands behind his head and leaning back in a swivel chair poised between the view of the street and the view of the avenue, "I am required to fly across the country, to our other coast. Those are long flights, and toward the end of them I look down at those vast, empty brown spaces, where nothing is, and I think, how *tragic* for our country."

On a less intimidating trip to Manhattan I caught up with a friend who taught and performed with the experimental dance troupe of Merce Cunningham. Recounting recent adventures, I pulled out a snapshot I had taken from a living room in Sedona, a view through junipers onto buttes of crimson and cream. My friend pushed it back like a trite postcard and said, "I can just see them on their sofa, admiring their model railroad scenery."

A more judgmental blow came from an elderly Romanian woman who, with her husband, had emigrated to the States in flight from German troops during the forties and had recently rented a car in Phoenix to explore the Southwest. "Scenery fortissimo, as you correctly predicted, but the people were immoral."

"Who did you meet?" I asked, alarmed.

"Meet? Who needs to meet? This is a world of suffering, darling, and people who hide from it by surrounding themselves with pink geology are shallow. And in this world of suffering, dear, shallowness is immoral."

I was glad the Romanian woman wasn't along when I drove to the Sedona airport, which sits on a mesa above the town and is known locally for its view. I stood at the brink, admiring a grander vista of the crimson and cream formations than I could glimpse from my friends' living room, and gaped as well at the motels, drive-in copy services, nacho nooks and view lots spilling southward, goring the valley. An elderly couple wearing cameras and carrying pop cans strolled toward me from a camper. "Where's Sedona?" asked the man.

"Sedona itself is that cluster of buildings near the cliff," I said.

"Then what's this down here?" he said, aiming a pop can at the strip.

"Just suburbia, I guess."

"Suburbia?" questioned the woman. "That's not on our map."

"What's there to see around here?" asked the man.

"The main thing is Oak Creek Canyon. That long red cliff, which is called the Mogollon Rim, runs across most of northern Arizona. A stream cuts a canyon straight into it for twenty miles to the north, and there are lots of trees—sycamores and oaks and various kinds of pine. If you look up, you can see different colored rock formations through the leaves. At the end there's a set of switchbacks to the top and a turn-off where you can look down on the whole canyon. There's a lot of traffic, but if you take it slow you'll enjoy it."

The man submitted to this speech, then stated, "We've already done that. What else is there?"

I thought hard. "There's a chapel built right on top of a rock. You might like that."

"That does sound interesting," said the woman.

"No, Gretch," he snapped, "we've already taken that picture."

Sensing a pure vein, I asked, "You folks are touring the West?"

"Les retired last year," said the woman, "and we thought we'd see the places we'd only heard of. We started in the north, Mount Rushmore and the Corn Palace. Then the Space Needle in Seattle, Crater Lake, San Francisco and Hearst Castle."

"We saw how they faked things at the MGM lots," he said, taking the thread, "then Disneyland, Yosemite, Vegas, Zion, Bryce, the Grand Canyon, and now we're here."

"And we'll be picking up Carlsbad Caverns on the way back," she added.

"Of all you've seen," I asked, "what did you like the best?"

They both fell silent, almost into a trance. "Oh," she finally answered, "it was all pretty much alike."

What follows, then, is culled from life among shallow, immoral people who inhabit tragic model railroad scenery that is all pretty much alike.

There Was a River

There Was a River

I

No one was willing to join my reunion. With a head full of old companions, I pulled into the Hite Overlook just as the sun was setting and the fins of sandstone below were losing their brick fire. Still further down, a more luminous formation was returning stored light in swirls of taffy. At the scene's bottom lay an alien substance: clear water. Its inlay of blue drove a chill between the layers of sandstone. By the water were other disparities: trucks, trailers, campers, and the scraped rectangle of a boat launch. The scene, however incongruous, should have been peaceful, but the rasp of a single motor filled the canyon rim to rim like an insect just out of reach. In the last light I crossed the blue fjord on a metal bridge and parked by the boat ramp.

I walked to the water, dipped my hand, smelled it, found it odorless. I proceeded up the ramp, past trucks and campers angled to enclose improvised patios where people nursed fires and beers, with radios playing softly and card games underway. The snarl of the one engine was everywhere, and to give my prowl purpose I tried to find it. The clamor was sourceless, but making my way through the clots of trailers I stumbled upon it. It was small, green, the size of a cocker spaniel. Electric cables bound it to a skiff with an outboard, and more cables looped from the skiff to a trailer. Something was charging something else, but I was less interested in the mechanics than in the fact that no one considered this din a breach of their nightfall.

The reason for this odd visitation was that it marked a thirtieth anniversary. On October 7, 1962, at a place near here also called Hite, three friends and I had embarked on what may have been the last trip through the Colorado River's Glen Canyon before the floodgates were closed at Glen Canyon Dam. I had known from childhood the spiky Sonoran desert of southern Arizona, but that float was my introduction to the smooth labyrinthine canyon country of southeast Utah. In a fevered mix of discovery and farewell, we traveled the riverscape at the country's stony heart, a pulsing lifeline that was about to be stilled forever. Three decades later, as the rest of the Americas and much of Europe prepared to celebrate or pillory the quincentennial of the arrival of Christopher Columbus in the New World, I had arrived for my own anniversary of an act in the conquistador tradition, the replacement of Glen Canyon with Lake Powell.

II

That I would go to Hite, population 2, on October 7, 1962, was determined in Aspen, Colorado, a backwater revenge on the conformist fifties. Of Aspen's bohemia, the most flinty and fearsome was Natalie Gignoux, owner of Aspen's only taxi company. Huguenot blood and a childhood in Maine forged this craggy featured, deep-voiced, hard-staring woman for whom nothing of significance occurred indoors.

When I dropped out of graduate school and found my own

level in Aspen, Natalie informed me that she and two friends
were looking for a fourth person to float for two weeks down a
stretch of the Colorado River called Glen Canyon. I had never
heard of this canyon, soon to be memorialized in a Sierra Club
book called *The Place No One Knew*, but I trusted Natalie's
taste in trips. The offer was one-time-only, because the entire
120 miles we would cover, as well as some miles we would
miss, were sentenced to imminent destruction by a dam. We
would be led by Katie Lee, a kind of Renaissance woman who
had honed her guitar-playing skills between takes during a
minor movie career, had toured America's leading nightclubs
interpreting songs that parodied psychoanalysis, and had become a pioneering river guide through both the Glen and
Grand canyons. I could come along if Katie approved of me.

I will never forget my first glimpse of Katie, on a jeep trip
Natalie had arranged for our meeting. I had expected an earth
person in the Aspen style, but under a straw hat with artificial
daisies Katie was blonde and trim, with the fine features of
the former starlet, emblazoned with raspberry lipstick, tan-
gerine shirt, lime green shorts, fuschia socks over her hiking
boots, and a tan that seemed to have depth as well as color.
This vibrating collage said hello appraisingly, as if measuring whether I could survive two weeks on a raft. Over several dinners and further jeep trips, Katie and I discovered
a mutual passion for books, puns, and subversive attitudes.
Under the pretense of giving up swearing, Katie would say
things like "Shit! I mean, hell," and routinely referred to the
Bureau of Reclamation, responsible for Glen Canyon Dam, as
the Wreck-the-Nation Bureau. I realized—partly by being referred to, occasionally, as "Muscles"—that what Katie wanted
in a fourth was a raft-loading, wood-gathering, pot-scrubbing
key grip, but I didn't worry about being miscast. The river
would sort things out.

It was three months after that first jeep trip that Katie,
Natalie, and I were tossing in a dusty Chevrolet the ten paved

and eighty unpaved miles from Blanding, Utah, to our embarcation at Hite. Sandstone, sagebrush, juniper, and piñon endlessly, kaleidoscopically refocused in erosional contours toward the Colorado River. Heaped about us were canned goods and a mass of neoprene rubber that was supposed to hold us up for two weeks. The road was an errant scar that presumably stopped somewhere. Near dark we rounded a crest like the others, and there was the legendary river—a span of muddy brown water easing between vegetation that radiated a vibrant, shocking green, the sort of color Katie would wear. We dropped into a dusky canyon, passing a small store and gas pump whose customers I couldn't imagine. Here, said Katie, lived one of Hite's two inhabitants. We drove another mile along tamarisk that hid the river and arrived at the two-room house of Hite's other inhabitant. Visiting that inhabitant was the fourth member of our party.

Leo Walter, a motorcycle repairman from Riley, Kansas, had been described to me as a river rat, so I looked involuntarily for the rodent—and found it. Though tall, with a face that stressed the vertical, his close-cropped hair and roundness of feature—including a small mouth with two prominent front teeth—added a woodchuck inquisitiveness and an uncanny resemblance to Humphrey Bogart. We were an implausible quartet, too tired to socialize just yet. Road-battered, we wolfed dinner and went directly to bed, Katie in a sleeping bag, Natalie in a brass bed under a cottonwood, Leo in the house, and I in a trailer in the yard. I had never slept in a trailer before but was too exhausted to feel claustrophobic.

In the morning, revived, I was better able to appreciate our host, who owned the little house and was the northern half of Hite's population. An electrician, mechanic, and assayer who worked at the Happy Jack uranium mine thirty miles back on the road we had just weathered, Slim was a laconic, square-cut man whose face was a motionless vessel for eyes that danced in endless blue detachment. Preferring solitude to the company of fellow miners, he fled to the river whenever he had time off. He allowed few guests in his hermitage: Katie was one, Leo another. Whenever Leo showed up from Kansas, he and Slim would take off to prospect for uranium and other ores, or to look for arrows, bowls, baskets, and spear points of a people who had vanished six centuries before. For Katie, Natalie, and me, despite our fondness for souvenirs, the back country was primarily scenery, a sensuous and aesthetic setting, and a strain of nature for art's sake colored our explorations. While Leo or Slim might register a "shore is pretty," mostly to humor us, for them Glen Canyon was foremost a springboard for adventures to be had while prospecting or looking for artifacts. They were not materialists in the sense that they ever expected—or even wanted—to get rich as miners or pot hunters; looking for treasure was an excuse to set out, to clear out the debris of assaying or repairing motorcycles by ditching civilization.

After omelettes that Katie turned out in Slim's kitchen, we took turns at a bicycle pump and watched the lump of neoprene lurch into a sixteen-foot raft like a hollow sea creature. When Slim started carpentering a wooden inner skeleton to support a thirty-five horsepower motor, I realized my skills weren't needed and set off for the little store. To my surprise, it also turned out to be a post office, officially called White Canyon, and its combination postmaster, merchant, and gas station attendant was a round little man with a jack-o'-lantern face named Woody. "Yeah, Hite's a real town because it's got a P.O.," he said, breathlessly. "But it was once a real city, mostly on the other side. Thousands of people. That was during the gold rush. Place was founded by a man named Cass Hite, in 1883, when he got this Navajo chief named Hoskininni to show him where the gold was. The gold was in the river. It was placer gold. Half the West got wind of it, and they rigged every kind of dredge to get at it. They put the town here because this is the best place to cross the river until you get to Lee's Ferry, and that's a couple hundred miles downstream in Arizona. Course, all the miners left when they got the gold out of the river. Some more came in a few years ago when uranium got a play, but that's about gone, too, except for the Happy Jack. The government put a road here in 1946. Goes clear to Hanksville on the other side, and I get the cars back and forth on the ferry."

"Katie told me about it," I managed to get in.

"Not too much business this morning. Probably okay if I leave the store. Wanna see it?"

Without my having to answer we piled into Woody's truck, which spat like artillery fire, and Woody maintained his chatter at the same tempo and a higher pitch. "Funny the government pays me to run a ferry when I can't even swim. There's a phone down there that connects to the store, so anyone who wants to cross can call me, but if they just stopped in the store in the first place, they wouldn't have to wait by the river. But people are crazy," he said, a statement I couldn't dispute.

We passed a cliff where a crank phone in a small box hung next to a large white arrow and letters saying FERRY PHONE. "You'd be surprised how many people can't find the phone," said Woody. Past the phone, the road ended at a contrivance like a lopped-off, one-lane bridge trestle with three World War II pontoons resting beneath it sideways. An engine pried from a Dodge truck hauled it along overhead cables salvaged from a mining operation. As Woody throttled the engine and we creaked and groaned to the other side and back, it struck me that a car improperly braked would roll forward or backward overboard.

Back in Woody's store I rummaged for something to buy while he kept talking. Among the postcards, potato chips, and cans of beans was a *Utah Historical Quarterly*, July 1960, an issue devoted entirely to Glen Canyon, perfect reading for the trip. "Good choice," said Woody. "Must have sold a hundred of them this year."

I returned to Slim's, admired the raft's new inner frame, then showed Slim my purchase and asked who Woody could have sold a hundred copies to.

"One hundred," said Slim, "is Woody's term for five."

"Do you spend much time with him?" I asked.

"Have you seen my shower?" asked Slim. I had indeed seen the spring-fed tank in the back of the house, with its spigot and its soap dish cut from a tire. "Whenever Woody wants to talk, which is all the time, and I hear that truck farting in my direction, I take off my clothes, turn on the spigot, and scream, 'I can't talk, I'm wet.' He probably wonders why I keep so clean."

It was now time to label the food cans with a magic marker so we would know what we were opening if the paper soaked off. Four successive cans of peaches were labeled Peaches, More Peaches, Still More Peaches, and Peaches Goddammit. A plastic lemon packed for making daiquiris was labeled Peach. When the raft and its contents were ready for the river, and the sun had disappeared over the rimrock, we squirted the false peach into a brew of rum, water, and honey—our standard cocktail for the next two weeks—and sang, after a Peter, Paul, and Mary tune currently popular,

Lemon tree very pretty
And the lemon flower is sweet,
But the poor plastic lemon
Is impossible to eat.

Since Slim was unable to come with us because of obligations at the mine, it seemed only fair to have one more rum with him after dinner. As we sat at the table and he and Katie traded tales of the river, a mouse appeared from under the refrigerator, tweaked its nose at us, and ran back to cover. Slim went to the other room, pulled a small .22 Derringer from his dresser, and returned to the table. We chatted with false nonchalance as Slim gestured with the loaded pistol. Fifteen minutes later, the mouse reappeared and in a burst of pistol shot it ran squealing to the porch. Katie followed and pronounced it dead. Slim blew softly on the smoking muzzle and drawled, "You know, I find this just the mousetrap for social occasions—after-dinner drinks, card parties and the like." His face remained stolid oak while his eyes flashed like sequins.

The sensation of actually being cast loose, afloat, escorted on hidden sinews of water, made even our last acts at Hite—loading the raft, saying goodbye to Slim—seem part of a lesser life. The outboard motor, powerful enough to take a light skiff wherever it chose, had little influence over our heaped scow, and only allowed Leo's hand to select which current to ride, which bank to land on. The inner skeleton that Slim had devised kept the mass rigid and prevented it from buckling in the middle, rather as if a fat woman had swallowed her corset. Though designed for ten persons, our gear under tarps had shrunk its free space until there was only room for two to sit on each side, on planks wound in canvas. Other choices were to clamber around the rim or jump in the water, which is what Katie did as soon as we were launched. Hardly beyond sight of Hite, she stripped to her turquoise headband, leapt yahooing like a Hollywood Texan, and churned delightedly through water as brown as she. Leo maneuvered the raft around, she drew herself in, and we shivered in her behalf. Katie, as we would see over and over, was impervious to the cold.

Thus began two weeks of variations on a single hypnotic theme. The riverscape, in essence, was simple. Water ran a rich silty brown between bright green banks of foliage, backed by walls of iron-reddened sandstone. The components of most landscapes are complexly interwoven, but here they had settled into layers: water, vegetation, rock, sky. It was within each layer that all was shift, transition, detail.

Days began when first light branded rimrock cayenne as the water surged a rich mocha. Sunlight crept down the walls, digging into bas-relief, trapping shadows between illusions of free-standing figures. Salmon, cinnamon, sienna, rust: the spectrum on the orange side of red varied as the day or the journey progressed, bleaching out as the sun climbed, deepening again as it neared the opposite rimrock. Against these reds hung desert varnish, tapering streamers of iron and manganese carried by rainwater over the rim, so dark that they reflected blue and unfolded like the wings of ravens. Following the river in lacquered fronds, they met the water with abstractions. Once sun hit the river, liquid silt caught the sky's blue, stirred it into coffee, tossed it back from sable, or blinded with scales of pure reflected light. Between water and stone lay the brief transition where talus had crumbled from the heights, thickening into loam for massive Fremont cottonwoods, delicate native willows, and invading tamarisk that lined the banks. Occasionally, when we floated near shore, a willow or cottonwood branch hung so close overhead that one could grab it, hang, and let the raft pass beneath, then drop into the water—a trick I considered but never tried.

The river engaged our eyes while subverting our other senses. Rich muds from mountain runoffs, particularly the basin's pungent Mancos shale, breached our nostrils with a sharp curry. While the Glen had no slathering whitewater in the manner of the Grand Canyon, even through the raft's blubber we could feel the current's slides and swells, meanders and eddies, muscular and insistent. Our ears were deprived of the river's slurpy silence whenever we insisted on steering, for the outboard forced us to communicate in voices pitched for hog calling. Fortunately, we spent only a fraction of our time trying to make miles down the river, and calm bested combustion. Calm bludgeoned its way into us, evicting clocks, lampooning our deadlines on the map, imposing a more sensible rhythm. Events remained sharp, but the days around them unraveled.

Having only seen beaches along the shores of lakes and

oceans, I was unprepared for stretches of soft, fine-grained sand, wide enough to set up camp between high watermark and vegetation, loose enough to blow into food and sleeping bags, sandbanks that waited each night to receive us. Willow and tamarisk islands were haloed with sand. Glen Canyon sand, like the sandstone walls above us, was variously tinged with red and strewn with the kind of whitened, silt-smoothed driftwood that urban rustics position on coffee tables. Scattered in profusion, they quickly filled aching arms on their way to the woodpile, from which we threw them on the fire like Philistines.

Our daily round, clumsy at first, turned by the end of the trip into a modicum of teamwork. We slept unencumbered by tents. Usually our first morning sound was Katie making an unwilling transition to consciousness with a series of small yelps like a strychnined coyote. Natalie, who slept by her camera, could be seen craning from her bedroll and peering through a lens, trying to catch the first photons nicking rimrock, or a fleeing heron. Leo, by stealth, had already gotten up and started a fire. I would be sitting up in my sleeping bag, getting a shirt on before I rose further into the cold, trying to make sense of what was going on. The first conversation was often generated by the first cup of coffee: *This brew has a hardness of seven. What did you use for a coffee pot, Paracutín?* And that old classic, *It's like the Missouri River, too thick to drink and too thin to plow.*

The fact that the women cooked didn't make it a man's world; the tenders of food were firmly in charge. Natalie's specialty was hotcakes bronzed in bacon grease. Katie's was omelettes improvised of, say, leftover ham in brown sugar glaze, cheddar cheese, oregano, basil, parsley, Tabasco sauce, and wild chives gathered on the riverbank, with eggs for a mere binder. Leo's and my specialties were obeying orders and staying out of the way. Leo had set up the kitchen the previous evening, moving heavy rocks for shelving and constructing a firepit for the grill. I washed dishes at the river, learning to use silt as a scrubber. After breakfast, we dismantled camp, folding canvas, stashing pots and plates. When we finally bore the cook box to the raft, it looked like an infant burial and felt as if the child had died from swallowing sixty pounds of lead. Our last act was to heave our garbage, tin cans included, into the river. As a puritan about littering I was shocked, despite Katie's assurances that the river, especially in the Grand Canyon, would grind, bang and pulverize everything to smithereens, whereas if we buried it onshore, it would only be dug up by coyotes. And if our garbage collected at the coffer dam that kept the builders of Glen Canyon dry, Katie added, it would serve them right for wrecking our river.

Once we had shoved off, Leo, a wizard at things mechanical, tended the engine and nursed the craft. Since I shared Leo's gender, it was assumed that I would share his practicality. A better dishwasher than stevedore, I was also obsessed with cramming all I could into a skimpy notebook. I would never be passing this way again—nor, alas, would anyone else—and my passion was to catch everything on the fly, even if Katie sometimes thought I blurred the line between scribbling and shirking. In the evening we reversed the morning routine, bearing the coffin out of the raft, spreading the kitchen canvas, gathering firewood. As we set up our personal areas, blew up our air mattresses with a bicycle pump, and pitched the communal kitchen, we managed to keep tabs on the sunset and down rum daiquiris from bright-colored metal cups. We used up the fresh meat and vegetables within the first few days, phasing in canned goods as we progressed.

Once dinner was consumed and the dishes washed, we heaped driftwood into a blaze and Katie brought out Freddie, her slightly undersized river guitar. In a voice that was intimate rather than powerful, and with a rich variety of effects on

Freddie, Katie sang, nearly to herself, old miners' poems she had set to music, as well as a repertoire generated during the previous two or three decades by a subculture of river runners who were busy creating new legends. Some ballads celebrated specific spots; others, with tunes and verses by Katie, mocked the Bureau of Reclamation. As if they foresaw the river's own end, the more serious songs were threaded by the image of ghosts: it seemed that everyone who had deposited a story along the Colorado, be it Indian, miner, or river runner, had left a spirit to haunt the waters and prolong an obsession. As flames danced luridly on the nearest canyon wall, sometimes kindling a glow across the river, Katie sang the story Woody had told me about the miner Cass Hite and the Navajo chief Hoskinnini. Into her setting in minor keys of a poem written in the 1890s, Katie had integrated effects on the guitar of galloping horses and the flowing river, with the ghost of Hoskinnini riding at midnight to guard the secret of a lost silver mine. Stars seemed to lean closer while a satellite, new to the heavens, cruised through them like a tour bus. Katie ended each ritual with a slow quatrain about riding a boat to the Other Side, after which we crawled into our sleeping bags and let the strum of the river carry us off.

Ostensibly on a river trip, our days were less filled with floating than with diversions on shore. Ruins, side canyons, mining debris, even historic graffiti provided excuses to beach the boat and prowl. We would be traveling 120 river miles, stopping well short of where Glen Canyon trips usually ended. We would stop short, too, of the eventual length of Lake Powell, because the construction of Glen Canyon Dam prevented us from reaching Katie's usual destination at Lee's Ferry. Due to the river's meanders, we wouldn't even cover 120 miles on a map. This shrinkage was, in fact, a release, allowing us to fall behind our own lazy schedule, to succumb to temptations along the bank, until it seemed to me that we proceeded as the crow flies—in circles.

With human history about to go under with the natural world, we picked over the remains of our own species—particularly the Indians who lived along the Glen and whose identity and fate are still being debated. They are now commonly known by the elegant term "Anasazi," a Navajo word variously translated as "someone's ancestors" and "ancient enemy." We used the slang term "Moqui," however, from a Hopi word meaning "dead," which has been preserved as "Moki" and "Mokee" in the names of motels and restaurants. For Leo, the hunt for Moqui keepsakes was the chief attraction of Glen Canyon, and he continually raked his eyes over the ledges, commenting, "Don't you spect Moqui Sam's been up there?" The plundering of Anasazi sites is now even more discouraged than the term "Moqui," but with all about to be drowned, even pothunting passed for archaeology and we rescued anything we could find. Our first stop, in fact, was less than a mile from Katie's swim, a Moqui ruin set in a canyon wall—a lost tile in the stone's mosaic, an introduction to the raiding of sites.

I tried, first from the *Utah Historical Quarterly* I bought from Woody and later from larger tomes, to get a grip on the Anasazi scenario, but it always blurred at the edges. Glen Canyon seems originally to have been settled around the time of Christ by the Basketmaker II culture. It amused me that archaeologists expected to find antecedants, to be called Basketmaker I, but that no earlier culture turned up, so that the first Basketmaker culture is officially Basketmaker II. The Basketmakers, primarily hunters, developed simple irrigation techniques and cultivated yellow flint corn, some squash, and some beans. Their first structures were pithouses, mere roofed-over depressions to store what they grew, a base for their wanderings. Small buildings gradually appeared, mere cubes of logs and mud mortar. The Basketmakers hunted deer and mountain sheep by spear and drew nets across narrower canyons into which they stampeded rabbits to be clubbed.

Through contact with the more advanced Hohokam and Mogollon cultures to the south, they acquired bows and arrows, axes and cotton, and gradually overtook their instructors. Now launched as the Pueblo culture, they flourished across the Colorado Plateau between A.D. 900 and 1300. With the development of pottery for storage and of improved irrigation techniques, they achieved the stable food supply that allows for leisure's by-product: civilization. Pithouses became kivas—smooth-walled chambers, often round, that served as clubs for men and sanctums for the practice of an unfolding religion. Decorated pottery and jewelry became intricate, inventive. The dog and the turkey were domesticated, though neither was eaten, and the latter provided decorative feathers. A most curious development was that the cranium broadened. It was thought at first that the narrow-skulled Basketmakers had been replaced by wide-browed superiors to the south. Later it was determined that cradleboards were added to the straps women used to lash children to their backs, pushing the young skulls forward and out.

While no culture in Glen Canyon attained the cultural summits found at Mesa Verde or Chaco Canyon, the river served as a kind of border where various groups mingled and hybridized on each other's fringes. Then within a brief period the Pueblo culture abandoned the Colorado Plateau, and by 1300 all caves and villages were left to crumble. The increasingly defensive nature of the late architecture—with occasional towers and the removal of plateau villages to caves—suggests invaders, perhaps Shoshonean marauders from the north. Compressed tree rings document a severe twenty-five-year drought just prior to 1300. Whether drought, invasion, overcultivation of fields, or a combination of the three, or even some other unknown factor, spurred the flight of the Pueblos is undetermined, but they resettled along the rivers of New Mexico and on Arizona's Black Mesa and remain one of our deep continuing cultures. Sun, wind, and predators like ourselves ply the remains.

Katie, Natalie, and I edged across a cliff to our first ruin and climbed to a loose-piled wall set back in the stone. After poking the ground and sifting the dust for nothing, I was disappointed to read in the windowsill of a wall an Anglo-Saxon name and a date—1946. Leo remained below, picking up a fine agate knife, discarding some pottery shards, and puzzling over a broken, double-notched, serrated piece of agate. "What is it?" I asked.

"I don't know," said Leo, "but when archaeologists don't know what sumpn's for, they say it's ceremonial."

Having expected to spend two weeks devoted to exploring the natural world, I was surprised at how much of our journey through The Place No One Knew was devoted to human folly, present as well as historic. During our first morning on the river, we had to douse a conflagration that leapt from the coals to the bacon grease while Natalie fought for every charred hotcake. As we pushed off, the propeller fell off the motor, and for the next half hour we waded the icy water scouring the bottom with our feet, performing a bump and grind through the ooze, covering the same area three times in vain while Leo installed our only spare. During our second departure, Nat's hat blew off, and though we retrieved it, we counted it as our third and final mishap.

Our own pratfalls were a good introduction to the day's major stop at Olympia Bar, where Hoskinnini had reportedly shown Cass Hite a deposit of placer gold to divert him from the silver mine. The gold proved so powdery it floated away in the water it was washed with. Strikes had played out in Colorado and California, however, and when Hite leaked word of the deposit to newspapers, miners with nothing else to do briefly converged on Glen Canyon.

Every manner of pan, sluice box, dredge, and hydraulic wonder was tried, with the maddest scheme hatched by an engineer named Robert Brewster Stanton. In the winter of 1889–1890, Stanton surveyed the entire river from Grand Junction, Colorado, to the sea and pronounced it suitable for a railroad bed. No capital surfaced for the project, but during the trip he met Cass Hite and learned of the placer gold. He thereupon envisioned a system of dredges powered by dams on the tributaries and the main channel, got backing, formed the Hoskinnini Company, and filed 145 claims over a distance of two hundred miles. From separate parts hauled over an improvised dugway he assembled his chef d'oeuvre— a hundred-foot scow laden with five gasoline engines, steel buckets, screens of increasingly tight mesh, devices for washing, amalgamating and retorting. But the gold was too fine, the scow stuck on the bottom, and the entire take, according to Stanton's diary, was $66.95. Stanton sold all he could salvage for $200, after an investment nearer $100,000, and left for other pursuits. But for sheer grandeur the escapade would not be equaled until the advent of the dam itself, beneath whose waters the scow's last splinter was doomed to rot.

As we scrambled over the remains of Cass Hite's mining operation at Olympia Bar, I couldn't help being struck by the difference between these remains from the industrial revolution and the nearly invisible relics of the Anasazi—even allowing that the most recent Anasazi midden would be six centuries older than the earliest ore crusher. Relics of mining eras depressed me anywhere, even in my hometown of Aspen, with their slag of physical ugliness and spent greed. Fortunately, the others were no more reverent than I, and we turned this one into a movie set. Leo, our Humphrey Bogart, was to play the part of a miner surprised to find a nude—

Katie—in his ore cart. As it turned out on the home screen, Leo ambles to the cart, claps his hand to his forehead with a self-conscious smirk, then saunters off without interest as Katie emerges like a Rhinemaiden stripped to her straw hat. It was, I thought, exactly what the spot deserved.

It wasn't until the third day that we explored the nonhuman and, to me, far more alluring world of the side canyons that frayed along the length of Glen Canyon, breaching stacked eras of sandstone. To reach them we usually had first to crawl and hack our way through stands of tamarisk, a ferny, cloud-like plant that turns from pale green to saffron in the fall. Imported from the Arabian peninsula during the last century to stabilize railroad embankments and to grace gardens, it had been spreading like a virus along the West's watercourses ever since, displacing native plants and tormenting people who wanted access to shore. In frustration I pulled at a shoot and found it connected to a root system like a buried road map. Within a year or two, such shoots grew into small trees that coalesced into fogbanks. Bloodied by this alien mist, we reached the entrance to Forgotten Canyon, so named because it was unaccountably omitted from the 1922 U.S. Geological Survey river map.

Threading Forgotten Canyon an easy half mile, we reached a set of Moqui steps. The phrase refers to any set of inden-tations chiseled ladderlike to get up an otherwise impassable formation, whether tooled by the Anasazi, miners, or cow-herds. Steps made by Indians were by far the most challeng-ing, being the steepest and shallowest and having received at least six centuries more erosion. Anasazi steps were also made for moccasins or bare feet rather than boots, and one set actually looked like it ascended an overhang. The steps at For-gotten Canyon had been cut by miners and gave firm traction to hands and sneakers. We were rewarded with a sweeping view of the river, as well as a pocket of sandstone rocks the size of golf balls, perfectly round, dark, hard, that sizzled into space when we rolled them over the edge.

Continuing past the Moqui steps, we entered a murky, mysterious cleft that countered the river's sunlit expanse. Sometimes these side canyons announced themselves with rounded portals, but more often stone merely parted, as if the cliff were left slightly ajar. As we advanced, the walls darkened and pressed closely around us. Dankness enveloped our skin and the damp sand, confined, steeped us in muskiness. In such constriction, the crunch of our boots grated in our ears so that we lowered our voices as one does, unbidden, in the shafts of cathedrals. Veering, doubling back, opening into amphitheaters that swelled with opalescence, pinching to our own width, these stone corridors forever promised further marvels, withheld their destinations, teased us onward. We balanced precariously over pools, waded icy water, anything to see one more configuration, to sample one more bend. Luring us even more than tight geology was light that trickled from a hidden sky. As it deflected from wall to wall, sometimes for 1,500 feet before it reached the canyon floor, turning sandstone incandescent, light took on a palpability of its own, as if it were finally not the illumination of walls but the revelation of some essence between them. We ourselves, lit on all sides, felt lifted into radiance.

After two or three miles, Forgotten Canyon shrank to an icy pool and we could proceed only by swimming. Leo reckoned he had come far enough, he'd set and wait; the rest of us stripped and plunged. The chill sped us to the far bank even as time was slowed by our agony. Beyond the pool the canyon widened to a river bank of willows and underbrush, and I learned a cardinal rule: never strip below the ankle. After a few minutes of walking on willow shoots, I felt I was treading broken glass. When we returned, failing to reach the ruin Katie had set as a goal, I was grateful for warm clothes. But if

I could have been issued only one class of clothing, it would have been shoes.

It seemed we could tie up the raft at any promising bank, crash through the tamarisk, and be guaranteed surprises. We picked a bluff whose wall was hidden by a stone shelf, recommended by its very anonymity. I was startled by a two-point stag, which gave me a flash of vanity because Katie had never seen a deer during her fourteen raptor-eyed trips down the river. Leo, ahead of us, stopped and leaned backward in precisely the pose of frozen shock we had aimed for in the movie sequence with the miner's cart. He strained until he broke his pose, gestured to us frantically, and two more deer leapt gracefully from beneath his perch. We watched the deer leap and freeze, leap and freeze, until they seemed to have disappeared. Several minutes later we glanced back and caught their heads arching regally over the current as they swam the river.

We climbed to Leo's perch and found the deer had been flushed from a clear emerald pool. Katie proclaimed it was movietime again, and we waited while she returned to the raft for the cameras. She arranged them to her satisfaction, stripped, and swam the icy water while we rolled the machines from above, ringed like med students in an operating theater.

Around the bend waited another surprise, an enormous, hollowed-out, three-quarter dome with a round hole in the top, a sandstone pantheon, plunging to irregular basins and whirlpools. Around the dome, a faint seepage sustained a band of maidenhair fern, a delicate frieze for a Pompeiian dining room. Invisible from the river, cool as a wine cellar, it made me realize one would have to walk both banks—physically impossible even if there were time—to claim full acquaintance with Glen Canyon.

On our return to the raft, we found another pool, and Katie instinctively jumped in. Natalie and I followed, and we finally wheedled Leo into joining us. He lowered himself inch by inch into the water while his skin turned from talcum white to glacial blue. Though freezing, he had the look of a Christian martyr being boiled alive. He endured immersion for two or three stoic minutes, emerged with a sick smile, and climbed into his sunlit clothes. We didn't make him swim again.

The fifth morning found us camping by a fresh spring that bubbled out of the rocks and sand, and we took advantage of an opportunity to do some laundry. We spread our clothes to dry on the raft rope, on tamarisk, and on a small yucca of the Utah canyons called Spanish bayonet. We then climbed a sandstone trail in back to check some ruins. When we reached the top, Leo, to our shock, pulled out the small Derringer with which Slim had blasted the mouse—and which Slim had traded for Leo's small telescope. To test the pistol's accuracy, Leo picked out targets below while we watched through field glasses to see if he found his mark. When we couldn't tell if he hit his targets, I suggested he take a few shots at my drying underwear. Alas, it was too far, and I lost a chance to get bullet holes in my shorts.

Katie, Natalie, and I swam from camp to an island Katie knew for its spectacular assortment of river rocks. Leo reckoned he would just poke around the campsite. Rocks heavier and older than the surrounding sandstone, washed from higher levels and tumbled smooth in the silt, had beached here cheek-to-cheek in exuberant mosaic. I collected a variety of Easter eggs, a small tugboat, and a fine acne specimen, all of which still grace my Aspen windowsill, mementos of an island now compacted under three decades of silt.

We swam back with our treasures in stuff sacks and displayed them to Leo. He admired them politely, then showed us what he had found—a Prince Albert tobacco can on a small stick, which contained a piece of lined paper on which was penciled (here somewhat condensed) the following:

COPY OF RECORD

NOTICE OF LOCATION

NOTICE IS HEREBY GIVEN, that the undersigned, having complied with the requirements of the U.S. statutes and the local laws and regulations have located 160 acres of placer ground to be known as the Oakes placer claim, situated in Kane County, Utah, and described as follows; beginning at the N.W. corner . . .

bug splatter

Located January 16, 1914

W. H. Shock   Elizabeth Talbot

more bug splot

T. E. Langford

Lou S. Hemenway

It was a claim made by the man for whom the bar was named, a significant historical document. The clear part was as legible as if drawn up yesterday, yet there remained hardly a vestige of lettering on the rusty can. For a half century the can had remained nailed upside down to a post, visible to all passers-by, but only Leo had bothered to look inside. Our rocks seemed less special, even as the river held our own facets to light: Katie was Impervious to Cold Water; I was Useless; Leo Found Things.

Since our arrival at Hite we had been contained by the river's field of influence—its flow, its beaches, its side canyons, its human history—and finally we climbed above it. What we found was nothing: nothing palpable, nothing made visible, nothing multiplied to vastness. For miles and miles we saw only sky and hellishly swirling stone. Here was a world as void as our imaginings of creation. It was inchoate with an angry beauty—as if a mad potter had whirled sandstone on spool after spool and set it spinning like gyroscopes out to a sandstone infinity. And in all this semblance of motion was something so still that it made us seem negligible, invisible, and immensely satisfied. That night, as if I needed to reassert my limits, I found a low overhang with barely room for my sleeping bag, crawled in, curled into the fetal position, and dove into a dreamless sleep.

After so much lateral dawdling, we knew that we had to make up some river miles. We broke camp early, then made three stops in the first mile: to photograph a Moqui pictograph, to get water, and to climb to a ruin that turned out to be a natural formation. Next came a debate about whether to explore Navajo Canyon: Natalie and I wanted to, Katie didn't, and Leo, ever deferential, refused to commit. After prolonged verbal eddies and undercurrents we could have learned from the river, Natalie and I prevailed without a formal vote. After frittering away the morning, we put on blinders, a sober mood, and charged thirty miles downstream.

Racing single-mindedly, we did notice two important changes. Instead of the autumnal calm we had enjoyed until now, we were buffeted by wind that drove icy waves into our pug-nosed craft and kept us cursing in a silence we occasionally broke, snappishly. When the San Juan, the major tributary the Colorado picked up on our run, joined us from the east, the banks suddenly reared higher, sharper, more dramatic. From our strategic campsite just below the confluence, we looked across at the highest point on the river, 1,200 feet of sheer rock from water to sky, without the ghost of a ledge, along with a circumference of bluffs, peaks, free-standing monuments, inaccessible caves. Our campsite was like a stage apron from which we could see, just downstream, what could have been the stage itself—two monolithic walls, between which smaller walls receded in tiers like scrims of scenery. While perhaps it was a place that cried out for tragedy, as Robinson Jeffers said of the Big Sur coast, what we got instead were field mice that lived under the inch-high shelves of our campsite. Running from their eaves of rock as if on wheels, they stopped dead, watched us quizzically with fat pointed faces, great ears, and eyes like beady black sunglasses, incessantly starting, stopping, scurrying back and forth importantly like little wind-up movie directors. They made pass after pass, closer each time in their game of chicken, then retired for the night just when we feared they were going to brave our sleeping bags.

On the seventh day we rested by not changing campsites. We crossed the river and Katie, carrying Freddie, led us into one of Glen Canyon's most revered features, Music Temple. Squeezing us claustrophobically, the canyon burst into a cavernous chamber from a brief, narrow canyon. Glazing its floor was a still pool that doubled the hemisphere of black rock, and the room's only exit was a cleft that began seventy-five feet overhead and climbed to the sky through hundreds of feet of twisting precipice. Because it was inaccessible, we populated it with secrets.

Music Temple's renowned feature, however, was not visual. Katie positioned herself against one wall and began to strum her guitar. The entire chamber seemed to vibrate, as if the strings were sections of an orchestra. Katie's voice entered and bloomed in its own timbre, unblurred by echoes and overtones. Like the light, the music came from nowhere, filling the walls with the body of its sound, as if Katie sang with the canyon's own throat. It struck me that with Music Temple and the Mormon Tabernacle, Utah had a primacy in acoustics, promoting what it manufactured, shrugging off what it was given.

We left the canyon, stashed Freddie, and began a long climb over Moqui steps and sandstone bluffs to the brink of the great precipice that faced camp. The ascent was easy, though at one point we did secure ourselves with a rope, and again we watched the horizon float toward an overworld of stone, strewn with pools that shrank and chilled in the short October days. Off to the southwest, like a stray Adirondack, rose the gentle, pine-covered slopes of Navajo Mountain, held by legend to be the source of local weather. We crawled on our bellies, queasily, to the verge of a 1,200-foot plunge to the river, a drop so sheer that by venturing our heads over the edge we couldn't see the bank below. Perhaps we were on an overhang that curved subtly inward. We dropped stones, quickly lost from view, and their reports were so faint we couldn't tell whether they hit land or water.

The scale of the country constantly baffled us, less because of its actual size than the freakishness of its smooth, sculpted shapes that didn't relate to anything we knew. Our camp was clearly visible below us, but how far was it? In pictures we took of side canyons, Moqui steps, precipices, and horizons of whorled sandstone, we nearly always included a member of our party to establish scale. But in the developed pictures the landscape still lacked scale, for the figure was out of context and merely seemed an artistic mistake. With solid walls instead of mirrors, Glen Canyon was still a house of illusion.

On our way back down Katie and Natalie climbed toward the back of Music Temple to see if they could peer into the chamber that hung mid-level, unapproachable from either end of the canyon. All at once we realized we were exhausted. Natalie started sliding on sandstone, missing occasional Moqui steps, making us all miss heartbeats. Even food and rum didn't revive us, and Katie, for the first time, was too tired to sing us an evening concert.

The change in the weather that had concerned us during our thirty-mile run caught up with us. A light rain fell in the night, and I learned my sleeping bag was not waterproof. Unwilling to face the day, I lay like a pharaoh embalmed in wet flannel. After breakfast, Natalie and I braved the elements up

Hidden Passage, a canyon invisible from the river because it threaded what looked from our camp like interlocking scrims of sandstone. Past the preliminary turns we faced a pool that filled the slot. Since it looked too cold to swim, we removed our shoes, socks, and pants, waded as far as we could, then edged with curled feet along the steep, slippery rock above the pool until it was again shallow enough to wade. Pleased with our agility, we sloshed through several more turns until we reached a pool with no climbable rocks. We balanced by turns on each other's raised, braced feet, peered around the next bend, took pictures that didn't come out perpendicular, then started back.

We reached the deep pool and with a boost from Natalie I started up the wall. I reached down to pull her up, and even with a precarious foothold I might have held on if it hadn't been for the muck on my feet. The pool bottoms, which had the consistency of poi, clung to my instep, and swishing my feet in water only made the clay stick the harder. I pulled Natalie's hand, she rose part way up, we tottered, she sank. With a chuckle she handed me her gear and clothes and swam the cold plunge. Garlanded from arms, shoulders and neck with her clothing, my clothing, cameras, light meters, seemingly every possession of value, I wobbled, feet prehensile with panic, along the ledge and to the exit side. We arrived at camp with fine silt stockings we could not wash but which in time dried so that we could chip off the crust like cheap ceramic.

Making river miles again, we retreated sullenly into ponchos as the rain resumed and thickened. We took a shore break and scrambled up a bluff, when without warning the sun came out. Every direction was steeped in its own set of colors. Toward the sun, rondures and domes were backlighted slate and silver into gleaming mosques. In the opposite direction, sandstone walls deepened to grenadine beneath a double rainbow. Navajo Mountain, baring ribs that belonged to no Adirondack, rose in glimpses between clouds trailing from a breast of down in the sky. Each direction competed with signs that the storm was over. But more storm clouds sent us to bed that night immediately after dinner, again with no concert, and we woke to a Scottish mist condensing to drizzle. Katie, discouraged, said, "I don't think this is a twenty-four-hour rain. I think this is a forty-eight-hour rain."

Leo looked at her blankly. "In thet case, I think I'll draw the string to my poncho."

Stalling for dry weather, we spread our sleeping bags under a broad dome and hiked a side canyon turn after turn, partly because one turn insists on another, partly to give our gear time to dry. We returned to find our bags as soggy and rank as before. Our obsession with the weather was diverted at a lunch stop downriver when we gazed at the opposite bank and spotted an enormous grayish-green rock, oval and vertical, poised on the rim. Binoculars revealed a strange lattice of cracks and canals. In a land where all substance above river level was sandstone, Elephant Ass Rock was a true anomaly. Katie swore that she was going to get up there the next day to figure it out. We didn't have time to mount an investigation, however, and we had to remind her that you can't expect to understand everything.

We were about to face another disagreement with Katie, this one about a possible encounter with our own species. Since we waved goodbye to Slim, we had seen no other human beings. Once when we were startled by a pair of horses, they were by association so like human beings that we inwardly jumped. Now we were approaching the canyon that led to Rainbow Bridge, the one well-known phenomenon within Glen Canyon, set in its tiny official national monument.

A man Katie had known from her years on the river, Art Greene, had been running tourist-boat trips sixty-nine miles upriver from Lee's Ferry to Rainbow Bridge ever since the late forties. When Glen Canyon Dam became a certainty, Greene adapted to the change by buying land Lake Powell would rise to meet, a holding that eventually became the Wahweap Marina resort complex. Meanwhile, he had bulldozed a twenty-mile road from Wahweap to Kane Creek, upstream in Glen Canyon, from which he took tourists on overnight trips to Rainbow Bridge. Katie had arranged for our own party to be met by one of Art Greene's employees at the trip's end, several days hence.

Natalie and I had never seen the world's largest natural bridge. The formation was so familiar from photographs that it was unlikely to spring any surprises, though Natalie and I didn't verbalize our attitude, we thought vaguely that we *ought* to see it, even if it lacked the adventure of the little-known side canyons. Katie, by small flippancies, let it be known that she wanted to sail on past the bridge. Natalie and I pretended not to hear her, Leo registered no opinion, and we steered the raft toward the campground. We faced man-sign in the form of two outhouses and a tent to house tourists for the night. We beached timidly downstream, and Katie went up to ask any guide she could find to tell our pick-up at Kane Creek that we would show up on schedule. We waited with misgivings. The outhouses glimmered ominously. Katie returned in silence.

"What news?" prodded Nat.

"There's two fat bitches, a drunk, and a screaming brat, and another party due at nine in the morning."

"Let's get outa here!" we replied in ragged chorus.

"Eeee-HAW!" shrieked Katie, who leapt, scissored, and fell back into the raft as we shoved off.

Sporadic rain persisted, redoubled, and rewarded us after the next breakfast when a waterfall leapt from a cliff across the river and was answered by a cascade from our side. Within minutes, shafts of water plunged from the banks upstream and down, leaping, tumbling, sliding, and arching in rust-colored profusion, their din blending stereophonically. Fresh water-

falls were born before our eyes. Suddenly, the rain stopped
and the falls disappeared as quickly as they had begun, a few
dwindling, the rest cut off as if by a spigot. We stood with rain
in our coffee, wondering if it had been a mirage.

A drizzle resumed, and rather than subject ourselves to the
river, we crashed through the tamarisk beyond camp to see
what entertainment the walls offered. So thick was the Arab
weed, drooping lugubriously, trickling raindrops under our
collars, slapping us in the face with cold sprays, requiring Leo
to slash branches with a hatchet, that we were disappointed to
find nothing but a small overhang too low to stand up under.
But it was dry, and with nothing else to do we began paw-
ing the dust. The charred soil yielded chips of agate: it was
a fresh Anasazi site, a spot so unpromising that perhaps no
one had looked at it before. Soon we were all scratching holes
like dogs, inhaling loosened dust. How many more sites were
tucked away like this, I wondered, condemned to be sealed
before they were even pawed at? Leo found a delicate bird
point, parts of spear points, parts of arrows, while the rest of
us found nothing but chips and patternless shards of pottery.
Natalie and I persisted, powdered with silt and the carbon
of old fires, but Katie slowed down, then threw a handful of
empty dirt on the ground and snapped, "I'm leaving."

I looked up, surprised. "Katie, you'll never make an archaeologist."

"Nonsense," she shot back. "I've had several."

The rain continued all day, and at last we dragged our
sleeping bags through the tunnel Leo had carved through the
tamarisk, lined them end-to-end in our trench of loosened
dust, and passed the night. It was tantalizing to consider we
were sleeping where human beings might not have slept for
seven hundred years, and might never again sleep.

For Katie, veteran of many such trips, and even for Natalie,
oriented from a previous river trip with Katie, Glen Canyon

was full of known formations, sandbars with associations, and islands with stories. In Katie's case, even names she gave to the canyons had stuck on the map. She knew when to anticipate tributaries, where to look up for granaries, and how to find Moqui steps behind the tamarisk. Since I had never been here before and couldn't return, I did not particularize to the same degree, and I let much of it run unnamed into a wash of sensation. There were side canyons I remember primarily for the way we got up them—by wading in ooze over our thighs so that each step gurgled as if we were priming a rusty pump. We crossed a pool by straddling a small plastic air mattress one at a time and riding it across like a drowning burro. Then we sent the mattress back to the next person on hand-beaten waves. Ideograms, better than English, might suggest such techniques as foot-feeling, crab-walking, bridging, spread-eagling, ass-wedging. We advanced sideways with our feet on one side of a cleft and our hands on the other. We boosted each other with hand stirrups, braced knees, and proferred shoulders as we scaled rocks, trees, and each other. There were mishaps: the time Natalie slid into a pool as if down a coal chute, the water lapping about her chin, her shirt ballooning like petals around her face, from which impasse she shot inexplicably back out like reversed film. Katie, climbing on the raft, grabbed in vain for the pole that stood on the bow, and pinwheeled into the river with arms and legs out like a starfish. Despite our pratfalls, by the end of our two weeks we moved like precision contortionists, knowing when to help and when to get out of the way. Our rewards were waterfalls, slots of amber musk, and domes that opened like stone's own chapel.

Just when we thought we had seen all the categories and the rest would be permutation, we would stumble onto something like the shelf of balanced rocks. I was familiar with that American classic, Balanced Rock, the boulder dancing on a pin, staple of jumbo postcards, pride of every state in the West.

I was unprepared for an entire shelf of balanced rocks no more than knee-high. Wind had eroded rotten sandstone beneath an assortment of granite, gneiss, and quartzite boulders, compressing the sandstone at their weightiest points and leaving them perched on finely whittled fingers. Some rocks stood on one leg, some on two or three, and sometimes a pebble was lodged, incredibly, between the sandstone peg and the boulder. Oblong, dark, river-polished, ludicrous, these balanced rocks were more like eccentric tea tables. Rotten sandstone, boulders, and evidence of wind could be seen in combination all along the river, and the variable that balanced them here escaped us.

Rain kept after us, holding back only to wallop again, and we adapted next by camping on a sandstone ledge beneath a roomy cave. There was no secret about this being an Anasazi site, for the Museum of Northern Arizona had dug here extensively, leaving its name and the number of the dig painted on the wall in white, along with an excavation hole for my ground cloth to dangle in. The weather let us dine on the shelf and settle into the cave with a welcome fire before it let loose again. A sound like far-off drums grew from our unconscious, then roared to a focus outside. "Flash flood," said Natalie. We knew nothing could touch our dry suspension, but it was hard not to feel threatened. Water suddenly pummeled the river just below us. We trained our flashlights toward the blast and made out a vague white blur. Katie and I put on our ponchos, advanced to where the water vaulted over the ledge, then picked our way to where the water landed. Out of the darkness seventy-five feet above us rocketed a shaft three feet thick, pale as moonlight, shuddering the soft clay beneath our feet. It was like standing beneath a giant turbine. Perhaps this falls was no greater than the ones we had already seen in profusion from a distance, but inching toward it close as we dared, feeling its mist filter up and soften our faces even as its energy plunged, we felt vulnerable, as if the ground beneath us might slide into the river and bear us away.

Turning to go, the water screaming at our backs, our cave glowed like a warm house on a wild winter night. Over the muffled roar of the falls, Katie sang her evening concert. We watched the embers die, heard the tumult diminish, drifted off to the rumble of the swollen river.

It seemed unreasonable that days without time could end, and the last day dawned spitefully blue and clear. This would also be the last day to compose a suitable end for that parallel trip, Katie's home movie. We came up with a scenario in which Natalie is cooking breakfast. The camera zooms in on the skillet, the spatula turns over a pancake on which is written THE END, Natalie flips it over her shoulder into the river, the muddy water washes over it and engulfs it as the writing vanishes. We fried a pancake until it was brittle, then wrote THE END on its less cooked side in magic marker. Then the camera began to roll. As the sequence turned out on the screen, Natalie, squatting at the grill, turns over a pancake that says THE END. She flips it nonchalantly over her shoulder into the river. The camera swings wildly, fishing for it, briefly locates it floating face down before it sinks.

Our last stop, Dungeon Canyon, was in its own way climactic. High water took us around the first turn by boat; then we waded in water to mid-thigh. The vaulting walls closed in, squeezing ever closer, letting only the faintest trickle of light ooze from the far sky while we filed through as phantoms. Ever more twisting and convoluted, the passage lengthened to a long nave of staggered piers in the style of late English gothic. There was no sound but the thread of our voices, our feet disturbing the pebbled floor, and the silence of eras gripped in stone.

The canyon opened for breath and closed again. Leo, shivering stoically, mentioned he was near the end of his trail, and we came to a pool. We all braved it and climbed at the far end into a cleft so narrow that we had to enter it sideways. Feet on one side, hands on the other, we ass-wedged over the deepening water until the canyon was the width of the human body, then thinner. The bottom lay fifteen or twenty feet beneath us, but there was no chance we could fall into it. At this compulsory stopping place, the stone hurtled upward at a mad slant, hundreds of feet, in parallels that nearly touched. Here it was always either dusk or night, and if there is consciousness in stone, this stone was insane.

From Dungeon Canyon to our getting-out point at Kane Creek we were in the autumn of our October trip. Regret at leaving the river—a river that always remained, in some part of our minds, a place to which we could never return—was suffused with a great peace. We looked back on our two weeks languidly, overfilled. We took pictures of each other, Katie and Natalie with scraggly hair, Leo and I with two-week's growth of beard. Natalie said that the reddish color of my beard proved her contention that I was a Titian; borrowing Katie's mirror, I thought I looked more like a teenage werewolf. But under our calm was dread—ultimately of the canyon's inundation, and more immediately of our return to humanity. We wondered whether the foursome Katie saw at Rainbow Bridge campground had been as terrible as she reported—perhaps she had even made them up—but they gave us an excuse to push on without having to associate with strangers. Even horses had spooked us. Whatever the tensions in our own foursome, we were used to each other, comfortable, xenophobic. The burden of small lies and adjustments that allows strangers to cooperate had been lifted, and though two weeks is a short time, we felt we had lost the knack. I even found myself timid about meeting the person Katie had arranged to pick us up.

As we approached Kane Creek, we lifted the glasses to see

whether the man with the truck had remembered. To our bafflement, the riverbank was swarming with activity pulsing in a nervous, metallic blur. As we came closer, the glasses picked up a disarray of trailers, construction cranes, shacks, trucks, and objects we couldn't identify, all in fitful circulation. In a spot destined to drown in a few months, why such frenzied activity? Had they moved the dam up here?

As the shore approached, more machinery took shape. The slope was covered with a strange growth. We beached and were instantly mobbed by a human cacophony: pink-faced men in straw hats and sunglasses, expressionless Navajos tugging on cans of Coors, overweight housewives with squalling children, tall Anglo men with beards, rabble that escaped categories. Cameras clicked in our faces. Had we crossed the Styx? Were these to be our hellmates?

A few gaped while the rest pelted us with questions. Where did we come from? Did we actually *float* down the river? From how far? Were we some kind of expedition? Was it dangerous? What did we eat? Is that a raft? What's it made of, rubber? To the last question, Katie snapped, "No, it's bacon rind."

Natalie managed to outshout them. "So who exactly are *you*?"

One of the bearded men replied, "We're filming the life story of Jesus."

At first it didn't sink in. We looked at the people, at the slope behind them where the curious vegetation resolved into plastic olive trees, then back at the people. "Yeah," said the man with the beard. "This isn't the Colorado. You just ran the Jordan."

We looked at each other with dawning comprehension. "Hollywood!" shrieked Katie. Suddenly we were all laughing. "Hey, which one of you cats is playing Je . . . ," I began when Natalie muzzled me from behind. Now everyone wanted to tell us about it at once.

"George Stevens, he's the director, went to look at the real

Jordan. It's just a pathetic little creek no one would believe, so we came here. The Colorado looks like the Jordan is *supposed* to look."

"Here's where we're doing the baptism scene, you know, when John the Baptist sprinkles water on Jesus' head. When Stevens first got here, he asked the ranger how deep it was, and before the ranger could answer, Stevens stepped in and disappeared. The ranger had to pull him out downstream."

"So they're building a platform underwater so that John and Jesus will only be in up to their waists."

We looked for our truck in this Biblical madness. Not seeing it, we started toward the boat ramp with the crowd surging after us, filling us with information. They were employed by George Stevens Productions, filming a best-seller called *The Greatest Story Ever Told*, cast of thousands, galaxy of stars. Navajos, always the bad guys, were playing the Philistines. "Has Charlton Heston finally made it all the way?" asked Katie.

"No," said someone. "This time he's doing John the Baptist."

"Is he here?" I asked.

"On this set we observe the Sabbath," said someone else, "and this is Sunday. He's off in Page getting a drink."

As we neared the boat ramp, through my mind floated a vignette in which Stevens was rolling the baptism scene while we floated into the background like an out-take from *The African Queen*. Suddenly, from behind a trailer, our truck materialized, and we shook hands with not one but two drivers, one an old acquaintance of Katie's. As we deflated the raft and loaded the gear, I hung my expired socks on a plastic olive tree, hoping to spot them later on the silver screen, but apparently they wound up on the cutting room floor.

We piled into a station wagon Art Greene had provided along with the truck, and Katie drove like an enraged bull past trucks and blondes in convertibles that cluttered the road Katie claimed as an extension of her personal river. Five miles out of Kane Creek we passed a forty-foot alabaster gate that rose starkly from the sandstone. "Walls of Jericho?" suggested Natalie.

"I think that's Old Testament," I said. "Maybe Jerusalem gates?" A few miles further we came upon a sugar cube village that could only be Bethlehem.

As we drove from filmland to Wahweap, I marveled at the shock treatment of our re-entry to civilization. We had dreaded contact with a driver who was there to do us a favor, only to be hit with artifice on a multi-million-dollar budget. Nothing but collision with the dam itself could have thrown our trip into greater relief. There was no overt connection between a dam and a film set, yet it was hard not to see them as pieces of a whole. That the film chanced to be the life story of Jesus only tightened the links, for what but the arrival of technology-driven Christian civilization from Europe led, nearly five centuries later, to the massive extermination of rivers and the mass hypnosis of the silver screen? And what was Katie's heavy foot on the accelerator—another artifact of technology—but a panicked flight from a culture that was desecrating all we had relished for the last two weeks?

Wahweap, showing little sign of the tourist empire to come, was a trailer court next to a landing strip where two tiny chartered planes awaited. Katie and Leo piled into one, Natalie and I into the other. It was late afternoon, with shadows blackening the canyons, scarring the plateau. We flew low, recognized a few places we had been, and screamed questions at the pilot over the motor's drone. The Henry Mountains, sharply divided between light and shadow, hung like model planets. In one short hour, flying a straight line, we sliced through what we had threaded for two weeks. Time and space seemed no more real than Hollywood. Suddenly we were descending into White Canyon, scaring a jackrabbit from the landing strip, unloading our gear, and watching the two little planes roar off.

Minutes after that we were having a bourbon with Woody in his store. Slim was off at the Happy Jack Mine. I sang a song I had made up on the plane, and all joined on the second chorus:

> *O little town of Bethlehem,*
> *How still we see thee rise*
> *Beneath the true and cobalt blue*
> *Of southern Utah skies.*
> *And in thy dark streets shineth*
> *Walls of papier-mâché.*
> *'Twas here that Charlton He-eston*
> *Was born on Christmas Day.*

III

It took twenty years—from the floodgate closing of 1963 to the flood year of 1983—for the lake to fill to capacity and for Glen Canyon to finish dying. Most who flocked to Lake Powell during the first years of its existence were people who regretted, mourned, or were enraged by the loss of the Colorado River. They were also impassioned or cynical enough to take advantage of the access that the rising waters gave them to previously inaccessible caves, ledges, and side canyons. For several years after our trip, Katie Lee explored side canyons in an outboard-powered skiff that seemed to be called SCREWDRIVER until you noticed a small gap between the *D* and the *R*, rendering it SCREWD RIVER. While I made numerous camping trips in the Utah canyon country with Katie during that period, I steered clear of Glen Canyon. I didn't want to bear witness to its end, and I put it off with the dread of being roused from a sumptuous dream. For some canyoneers, Lake Powell was simply a truce with reality; for others who discovered Glen Canyon

after it had already begun to fill, it was a series of fresh adventures in a new country, new every year as the reservoir
rose.

A particularly acute observer of the filling of Lake Powell
was Remo Lavagnino, whom I met in Aspen a decade after
my trip through the Glen. He had first reached Glen Canyon
in 1963, the year the water started to back up. Pulling into
Wahweap in the spring of 1963, he rented a rowboat with an
18-HP outboard from Art Greene and motored to the mouth
of the Escalante River without encountering another soul. He
and three friends then chipped in on a boat, kept it at Wahweap, and returned to it yearly. The lake was still a mere
bloated river and the people were like river people, mostly in
kayaks and canoes. His party documented further ecological
and archaeological losses as the lake rose.

In a cave up the Escalante River, for instance, Remo found
a rock inscribed, in script, "In Search of Nemo." The ref-
erence was to Everett Ruess, a twenty-year-old poet, artist,
and desert explorer who disappeared in 1933 and had been
the subject of a nationally publicized unsuccessful search. He
had sometimes called himself Nemo, classical Greek for "no
man." Inscribed in the slickrock of the same cave was another
message about Nemo in French, which Remo couldn't read.
Never having heard of Everett Ruess, Remo was startled by
the similarity to his own name, as if someone had been search-
ing for *him*. Knowing the rock would be lost under the water,
but fearing it would capsize his low-sided, overloaded boat, he
stashed it upside down at the back of the cave with the intention of returning for it later. When he returned with a lighter
load, the rock had vanished. Someone, he assumes, still has
the rock, while the French inscription lies buried under Lake
Powell.

When the lake level had reached some seventy-five feet,
Remo took his boat into the drowned hemisphere of Music
Temple and stepped into the cleft that had seemed, in 1962, a

nearly imaginary canyon, one that Katie and Natalie had only dreamed of entering. To his astonishment, his party found a ledge barely protected by an overhang, full of artifacts from the pre-ceramic Basketmaker III culture. "We found moccasins, atlatl darts, quids, which were bits of yucca that had been chewed and spit out like tobacco, and a twilled ring basket that was in perfect shape. We didn't know what much of the stuff was when we found it, and half the fun was going to museums later and identifying it by matching it up with known objects. My twilled ring basket is better than the one on display at Mesa Verde. We played in that spot like it was our private sandpile. When we came back the next year, it was ten feet underwater, and everything we hadn't taken was gone."

As the lake rose and spread, Remo and friends noticed a change in the craft they encountered. There was a phase of tiny one-man skiffs, precursors of wind surfers, tacking back and forth in the widening waters. Then came the larger inboard motorboats, models that got bigger with each passing year. During this period, Remo's group was aware of accelerating erosion. Most dramatic was the undermining of sand hills that leaned against cliffs at the angle of repose and collapsed into the lake, creating round, sudsy lagoons and leaving scars where they had shielded the walls. Remo's party, camping well above the waterline in case the lake rose in the night, lay in their sleeping bags and listened to the roar of sand collapsing. By day, they saw rocks turn into islands, trapping animals. Remo found, as if in a fable, an entire island full of mice running around frantically as the water rose. When he returned later in the day, the island was gone. He saw a racoon marooned on a ledge in a box canyon. When he saw his first rattlesnake in the wild, it was on a sandbar in front of sheer walls, with nowhere to go.

Remo's group would have kept exploring in the low-slung boat, but each year the lake seemed more dangerous. Waves smashed the cliffs and rebounded with no shrinkage in size. There were swells and whitecaps, and the kayaks and canoes had disappeared. As the wind whipped the ballooning water into wilder, more unpredictable tossings, the boats grew until they were yachts and houseboats, with dinghies for plying the side canyons. Watching watercraft broaden was like watching nonbiological evolution. Remo dates the last of his Lake Powell to a particular moment when he saw what looked like an armada bearing down on his party's frail skiff. They stared until they realized it was eight speedboats in a row, each pulling a waterskier who veered back and forth in what seemed an advancing net. "That was the end of our Lake Powell, which was a place for exploration, and its conversion into pure recreation."

By avoiding Lake Powell entirely, I missed Katie's confrontation with the loss of her river. I could only wonder that she subjected herself to that loss. Natalie took one trip with her in SCREWD RIVER, motored over Moqui steps they had taken, powered into Music Temple, and Natalie couldn't face it. "You could take a motorboat right into the place where we had spent the night in the thunderstorm," she complained. "My favorite places were just devastated." They took SCREWD RIVER as far into the side canyons as they could and hiked what was left, leaving the boat mired in a phenomenon known as Dominy Stew, after Floyd Dominy, the feisty chief of the Bureau of Reclamation. The recipe varied, but the daily special might include dead trees, outboard motor oil, styrofoam cups, filter tips, film cans, rotting animals, and the kind of mud we had once tried to claw from our legs. Natalie remembers returning from a hike, coming upon a boatload of fishermen tossing cans overboard, and Katie yelling, "Sit on your ass and catch some bass." Katie doesn't recall the incident but says that she remembers she snapped, "Up yours, dipshit!" to a drunken fisherman at Hall's Crossing with a bitterness the man may not have connected with the loss of Glen Canyon.

After her one trip in SCREWD RIVER, Natalie didn't return until nearly ten years later when the lake was almost full and didn't remind her of Glen Canyon. From 1972 to 1975 she was part owner of a boat at Bullfrog Marina, and she, too, found the lake dangerous. "It was fun but scary. The lake gets the big roller kind of waves. When it's acting up, you'd better just head for shore." It was during that period that all from Aspen who frequented Lake Powell were sobered by the fate of a deliveryman for Railway Express named Ken Ward, who had moved to Lake Powell to run the ferry between Bullfrog Marina and Hall's Crossing. No one ever quite understood what happened, but it was at night and there was a storm. Ken was alone on the ferry. The ferry was found the morning after the storm in battered condition, and Ken was never recovered.

Of the four of us who took the trip through Glen Canyon in 1962, Leo was the least affected emotionally. In fact, he didn't wait for the rising of Lake Powell to seize an opportunity. As soon as we had flown back to Hite, he took off in his Willy's for the set of *The Greatest Story Ever Told* and offered his services as an extra. "They dressed me in this fancy sheet and made me a stand-in for one of them whatcha-ma-callits that trails after Jesus."

"An apostle?" I asked.

"Yeah, an apostle. It was colder'n hell and we spent most of the time in our sheets standing around fires, burning on one side and freezing on the other, then turning around to even it up. Everyone had the flu, and pretty soon that included me."

Leo did return to the area to take more trips with Slim to prospect and look for mementos of Moqui Sam. Then he took up jade hunting in Wyoming and discovered the second largest piece of jade ever found in the United States, 2,200 pounds, for which he found no market because it lacked the cachet of Oriental jade. As to whether he felt the loss of Glen Canyon, his only reaction was, "Boy, all that new water was really sumpn." His friend Slim, however, had considered the river his refuge. As the lake rose he was forced to move into a trailer at Fry Canyon, a tiny settlement near the Happy Jack Mine. But he was not about to let the lake take his two-room house piecemeal, and as the water crept toward its foundation, he dynamited it.

No matter how bitter we felt about it, there was no avoiding Lake Powell, for the Colorado River drained the canyon country of southeast Utah, and if you followed those canyons downstream, they delivered you to the lake. I had my first encounter with Lake Powell in 1977, at a reunion of sorts fifteen years after our float through Glen Canyon, for the trip included Katie and Leo, and Slim was to collect us at Lake Powell in his motorboat. We lacked Natalie, who had incomprehensibly defected to the game of golf, but we had gained Remo and his friends. I hadn't seen Leo in several years and was startled when he walked into the Elk Ridge Cafe in Blanding. He had acquired four new pearl-like upper front teeth that he referred to as "mah toof," giving his own larger teeth to either side the look of fangs. Excited about a new fire starter that involved a kind of brass knuckle, flint, and some exotic tinder from Mexico, he lit a small pile of napkins on the tabletop. At the age of sixty, he was still the same Leo.

For the following ten days we marched through sand that blew like white scarves down a usually damp drainage while swollen indigo clouds threatened but never delivered rain, and we were finally rewarded with idyllic limestone pools. On the last day we dealt with a tortuous descent. Rounding a bend, we came upon a stretch of shelves strewn with sticks and dirt as if ravaged by a clearcut. Lake Powell had risen here, deposited its gifts, and left. Around another bend was a rancid exhalation, a mudbank with bleaching cola cans and torn jeans, and an arm of water whose shade of green had recently been featured in *The Exorcist*. Beyond it stood Slim— his eyes glittering, his square features suppressing a grin—

offering cold beers out of his tethered boat. We loaded quickly and roared into Lake Powell. Canyon walls of the sort we had just labored past with forty pounds on our backs, our very slowness compelling us to study them, flashed past like dioramas in a museum. Suddenly the sky that had withheld its moisture for ten days let loose. Lightning cracked, thunder tore through the motor's racket, and we crouched under ponchos that left only tiny folds to peer from. All I could see was the outboard itself, which, I noticed to my amusement, was a Johnson Thunderbolt. Having put it off all these years, skimming, miserable, and cold, I was baptized by Lake Powell.

The enormity that two hundred of the most beautiful river miles imaginable could be erased by one wedge of concrete has taken three decades to realize. To blame the "Wreck-the-Nation Bureau," a federal agency whose highest goal has become self-perpetuation, is too easy, too like blaming the trigger finger without questioning the brain. Even for Katie, with enough rage for all antagonists, there was a sense of bafflement, of an enemy too amorphous to target.

I made my first attempt to understand it on the river itself, reading—by flashlight in the sleeping bag, in the few moments before exhausted sleep—the *Utah Historical Quarterly* I had bought from Woody. Devoted entirely to Utah's stretch of the Colorado River, it was written by biologists, historians, and reclamationists, with an introduction by the current governor. One article would hail the replacement by water of what another had just praised. The conclusion, with mock objectivity, described "testimony generated by national conservation groups" as "bitter and emotional," while "successful efforts to secure authorization" for the dam were "an outstanding example of organized effort" by "nationwide information campaigns." Schizophrenia paraded as scholarship.

As I read more afterwards, a scenario emerged. The drainage basin of the Colorado River includes portions of Colorado, Wyoming, Utah, New Mexico, Nevada, Arizona, and California, and each began claiming its perceived share of the Colorado River from the moment of statehood. California, with its rich Imperial Valley near the Mexican border, first established a major irrigation canal. The upstream states panicked and demanded that their own water rights be established. A flood that began in 1905 and raged for sixteen months through California farms and homes—breaking through the canal that fed the Imperial Valley, creating the now toxic Salton Sea—set off a howl for flood control dams. In 1922, a pressured Congress instructed Secretary of Commerce Herbert Hoover to hold public hearings in all states involved, and the emerging Colorado River Compact was ratified. A kind of legal parting of the waters, the compact divides the river at Lee's Ferry, at the beginning of the Grand Canyon, and awards an equal 7,500,000 acre-feet to the upstream and downstream states.

The Lower Basin plunged into action and completed the massive Hoover Dam in 1935, creating Lake Mead and sending power and irrigation to southern California. The Upper Basin states watched hungrily, bickering among themselves on how to carve up their half of the water. The Bureau of Reclamation, impatient for contracts, came up with the Colorado River Storage Project and Participating Projects, with four major dams—one being Glen Canyon—and eleven minor ones. They were calculated to placate all parties, including themselves. Touted benefits included hydroelectric power, flood control, irrigation, recreation and—incomprehensibly to some—scenic enhancement.

When the plan hit Congress, not all were placated. Chief opposition was led by conservation groups because one of the projects, Echo Park Dam, was located in Dinosaur National Park. Seeing a potential threat to the entire park system, the conservationists opposed it as a dangerous precedent and

achieved what may be the first nationally consolidated con-
servation victory. Echo Park Dam was relocated to Flaming
Gorge, outside the park, and language was inserted in the
Colorado River Storage Act stating: "It is the intention of
Congress that no dam or reservoir constructed under the authorization of this Act shall be within any National Park or
Monument." Almost all of southeast Utah, including Glen
Canyon in its entirety, had once been proposed for protection
by Franklin Delano Roosevelt's secretary of interior, Harold
Ickes, but the proposal never passed Congress. As unthinkable as it is in retrospect, Glen Canyon was never defended
by conservation groups because it had never been included in
the national parks and monuments system. The Sierra Club
and its allies were so intent on defending what had already
been set aside that their only objection to Glen Canyon Dam
was that it would back water into the tiny Rainbow Bridge
National Monument. Seeing another threatening precedent,
they proposed a retaining dam to protect the monument—
even if that dam overwhelmed what it protected. The conservation response to the Colorado River Storage Act was entirely
legalistic. It seems no one of consequence ever ventured to inspect what would be flooded, apparently assuming that if the
area were so worth preserving, it would be protected already.

By the time the Storage Act passed Congress, it had swelled
even beyond the Bureau of Reclamation's own dreams. Arizona wanted its own subsystem, Colorado wanted another, and
each state appended projects like tipplers buying each other
drinks. The whole concrete folly was chaperoned through
Congress by Wayne Aspinall, who was for twenty-four years
a congressional representative of Colorado's Western Slope,
and for twelve of those years the powerful chairman of the
House Interior Committee. The dam-loving Aspinall was particularly galling to river lovers from Aspen because he was our
very own Congressman. In 1972, we took revenge by helping a

law professor knock Aspinall out of Congress in a Democratic primary.

In October 1974, when Morris Udall was contemplating a run for the presidency, his brother Stewart, who was secretary of interior under Kennedy and Johnson when Glen Canyon went under, came through Aspen on a fundraising trip. I was anxious to learn what I could from one of the players, and I volunteered to drive Udall back to the airport. After answering Udall's questions about the difference between our high-altitude narrow-leaf cottonwoods and the canyon country's Fremont cottonwoods, I plunged in. "How did Glen Canyon Dam come to be? Can you tell me something of what led to its construction?"

"Well, I voted for the goddamn thing when I was in Congress," he replied in a flat, borderline sarcastic tone. "And I floated the whole Glen in 1960. There wasn't the feeling about dams then that there is now, nor the strength in the environmental movement. Goldwater had been through the Glen and voted for the dam, and he is against dams in the Grand Canyon now. The place was hard to defend because it was really unknown. Only a few hundred people—maybe a few thousand—knew about it. The book was right—it was really the place no one knew."

"Weren't there any alternatives?"

"There were other dam sites, if that's what you mean. They were all bad, of course. One site they talked about was below the confluence of the Colorado and the Green. The trouble with Glen Canyon Dam is that the river is so flat through there that the reservoir backs up for two hundred miles."

"What part did the Sierra Club play in the decision?"

"I'm afraid the Sierra Club must share some of the blame. They put all their strength in the fight against the dam at Echo Park. They had the idea from John Muir that parks were the thing, and had to be protected. Glen Canyon was much *better* than a park, but it wasn't a park. So they used up all their strength fighting the Echo Park dam, and, of course, in protecting Rainbow Bridge."

"Didn't they want to build a dam to protect Rainbow Bridge?"

"Dumbest goddamn thing I ever heard of. Anyone who really cared about Rainbow Bridge had to be against that. The monument is just a 160-acre box on the Navajo Reservation. I had to decide against them on that one. If they really wanted to save Rainbow Bridge, they should have fought Glen Canyon Dam."

"If the Sierra Club had fought Glen Canyon Dam instead of the dam at Echo Park, could the canyon have been saved?"

"It would have been a bloodier showdown."

"Hasn't David Brower had some second thoughts about the Sierra Club position on that?"

"Yeah. Dave once told me it was a mistake."

"But you favored the dam. . . ," I persisted.

"When I ran for Congress twenty years ago, dams were the great thing. California was stealing our water, so we needed the Central Arizona Project. Aspinall wouldn't let us have it unless he also had his Upper Basin dams. Of course, he wanted dams at Echo Park *and* Glen Canyon."

I came now to the question that most bothered me, the one that no one seemed to ask. I could understand the case being made for dams in terms of power generation, flood control, and irrigation. I could see that recreation is used as a selling point, and while the bathtub rings of *all* reservoirs negate, for me, their scenic value, I also know that tastes in scenery vary. What I did not understand is why a state, or group of states, needed to impound water physically, merely to stake a claim. Water-measuring devices are sophisticated; laws can be passed giving credit to any state for the acre-feet it deserves; there is no reason I can conceive of why a geographical entity needs to impound water *bodily* to assert its rights. Yet

even now, officials in my home state of Colorado argue that
we must build more dams—drowning bottomland, destroying riparian zones—so our archenemies in Utah and Arizona
won't steal our precious snowmelt. With such thoughts in
mind, I asked Stewart Udall, "Couldn't they just measure the
amount of water that passed Lee's Ferry and give the Upper
Basin *credit* for their half of the water?"

"Sure," he said. "There were lots of other things that could
have been done. But Aspinall wanted dams. He said that not
to have dams would interfere with their bookkeeping system."

We had reached the airport. Udall thanked me, grabbed his
bag, and ran for his plane while I sat in the jeep, playing and
replaying the phrase, "not to have dams would interfere with
their bookkeeping system." To preserve a bookkeeping system
we are willing to destroy an ecosystem.

As millions who have never heard of Glen Canyon converge
on Lake Powell for motorized recreation, and hydroelectric
power fuels the epidemic of ranchettes around Phoenix, Glen
Canyon Dam may seem to have silenced its long-defeated
critics. Such acquiescence has not been smooth, however, for
the dam has since risen as a central symbol of all we have
done wrong in breaking the West.

Least heard in this country are complaints from south of the
border. Most of the Colorado River has now been stoppered
into a string of lakes, each one silting up, and none of that
silt now reaches the mudflat that was once the teeming delta
of the Gulf of California. The gulf, still possessed of more
species of aquatic life than any comparable body of water in
the world, no longer receives the Colorado River nutrients that
form the base of its chain of life. I once crossed the Colorado
River on the southernmost bridge before it reaches the gulf
and found it smaller than the creek that flows below my cabin
in Aspen. Most of the time, I am told, the mighty Colorado
doesn't reach the sea at all, for what is stored behind dams is

shot laterally through the canals of the basin's seven squab-
bling states. Mexico has been pledged a certain percentage of
the water by treaty, but what it receives is so far below the
legal amount, so ruinously salty for its fields, that the country
has repeatedly sued. The Colorado River has been frequently
and accurately compared to a massive and botched system of
plumbing.

More visible to Americans has been the effect on the Grand
Canyon, which begins only a few miles downstream from the
dam. It isn't merely that the water, previously warm and rusty
brown, now runs blue and cold. In a double attack, the river
no longer bears silt for the Grand Canyon's beaches, and the
dam's discharges have been regulated to reflect power de-
mands hundreds of miles away. When Phoenix or Las Vegas
wants heating in the winter or air conditioning in the summer,
discharges can be adjusted minute by minute to shoot instant power through cables. Instead of the natural cycles that
rhythmically built the Grand Canyon's beaches and flushed
them clean, discharges have lurched from between 1,000 and
31,000 cubic feet per second in a single day, raising or lower-
ing river levels violently in the process. Such a system ravages
the riverbanks of the Grand Canyon, undermining its indigenous plants and animals. It has also collided with increasingly popular float trips through the Grand Canyon, which
use those beaches as campgrounds. In October 1992 boat-
ing companies, their clients, and conservation organizations
finally won passage of the Grand Canyon Protection Act, di-
recting the secretary of interior to manage discharges so as to
preserve the natural and cultural resources downstream.

As backpacking flourished in the 1960s and 1970s, and
more and more people discovered the joys of exploring the
canyons surrounding Lake Powell (often descending them in
bliss only to be stopped by the lake), Glen Canyon became
more famous in death than it ever had been in life. Lake
Powell, or its equivalent in mines, power plants, new roads,

and nuclear dumps, was exactly what converted desert rats didn't want to happen to their favorite canyons. Environmentalists successfully defeated more coal-fired power plants and a nuclear dump. Politicians and federal land agencies successfully fought off wilderness proposals, and nearly everything that affected southeast Utah wound up in court.

Besides backing a lake into the canyon country's very heart, two related phenomena have elevated Glen Canyon Dam into a symbol of mindless ruin. One phenomenon is its literature, first the Sierra Club memorial photo essay on Glen Canyon, *The Place No One Knew*, then the creations of Edward Abbey. In the essay collection he became known for, *Desert Solitaire*, Abbey recommended blowing up the dam, and in *The Monkey Wrench Gang*, his later popular novel of environmental sabotage, or "ecotage," the exploding of Glen Canyon Dam became the book's elusive Grail. In other writings, Abbey made a more interesting suggestion that the water be allowed to flow around the dam and that the structure be left to stand as a monument to bureaucratic stupidity.

The works of Abbey largely inspired the second phenomenon, the emergence of the radical group Earth First!, connoisseurs of ecotage. Earth First! pulled off an inspired piece of political theater on the first day of spring, 1981, when they stood on top of Glen Canyon Dam and unrolled a three hundred foot strip of black plastic that looked like a massive crack. The cracked dam has been a staple of T-shirts, along with a more explicit image, taken from a later Abbey book cover, of the river leaping through the dam like a wild animal out of a cage.

Katie Lee spurred the anti-dam sentiments whenever possible. She appeared at environmental rallies and campouts, many of them by Earth First!, singing the songs I had first heard on the Glen and that she had put out as a record and later a cassette. She has also continued to rework an unpublished autobiographical novel about her earlier trips through

Glen Canyon, showing the effect of the dam on her charac-
ters, called *All My Rivers Are Gone*. If it's ever a hit, I have
suggested, she should have a natural sequel in *All My Lakes
Are Fake*.

Like many diehard canyoneers, Katie has her own fantasies
of blowing up the dam. Afflicted with a terminal disease, she
would strap a bomb to herself, take the dam with her, and
ride the river to the Other Side. The closest she has come to
detonation was at a birthday party I threw for her in October
1975, an affair that doubled as a farewell to a louse-gray carpet that came with my house. Two friends sculpted a chocolate
box cake into a reservoir of runny chocolate pudding behind
a dam of vanilla wafers. My first thought was to provide a
tiny firecracker Katie could actually light. As I brooded on the
parts of the house not to be replaced, on the guests' corneas,
and on my own liability, I decided to leave the destruction of
the dam to Katie's instincts.

Katie arrived in a riotous floor-length gown she had sewn
from multi-colored patches, a kind of bedspread with cleav-
age. Glen Canyon daiquiris were downed, Katie pulled out
Freddie and sang river songs, food was dispatched, and as
the guests croaked Happy Birthday, the cake was deposited at
her feet. Kicking off her high heels, lifting her dress to reveal
what she often referred to as "the essential Katie," she sent
her right foot through the wafers and shrieked, "Take *that*,
Wreck-the-Nation Bureau!" Chocolate ran like magma onto
the doomed carpet. To cheers from the guests, Katie leapt into
the middle of the cake, held her hem high, maintained a vol-
ley of Hollywood Texas whoops, and danced like a peasant on
ripe grapes. By the end of the party, the floor looked like a
dig by the Museum of Northern Arizona, and if it had any relation to what would happen if the plug were pulled on Glen
Canyon Dam, Glen Canyon would not now be a pretty sight.
Next morning, as I was soaping glasses and nursing a hang-

over, the carpet installers called to inform me that my order would be delayed six weeks, and I was stuck with my own little parlor of Dominy Stew.

The absurd causes and warring consequences of Glen Canyon Dam have been best caught for me in a 1970 film, *Planet of the Apes*. In the opening scene, Charlton Heston arrives on a strange planet I immediately recognized as Lake Powell through a red filter, and I was amused that Heston, having left Glen Canyon as John the Baptist, had returned to Lake Powell as a space traveler. Still more fitting, the strange planet turns out to be Earth after all, in the wake of a holocaust. There had been books explaining the holocaust of Lake Powell, from the jeremiads of Edward Abbey to a fascinating book by John McPhee, *Encounters with the Archdruid*, in which he lures the Sierra Club's David Brower and the Bureau of Reclamation's Floyd Dominy to float together through the Grand Canyon while duking it out verbally over Lake Powell. It wasn't until the publication in 1989 of Russell Martin's aptly if wrenchingly titled *A Story that Stands Like A Dam* that the entire saga—of engineers and bureaucrats as well as politicians, environmentalists, and river rats—is laid out in full, leaving me, at least, wanting no more. Still the story of a holocaust, *A Story that Stands Like A Dam* is *Planet of the Apes* without a red filter.

Ever since the floodgates closed conservationists have been trying to get what's left of the canyon country into wilderness designation. They unsuccessfully sued to keep the lake one hundred feet below the level of the dam, technically to keep water from invading Rainbow Bridge National Monument, more broadly to protect all the canyons that would be similarly shortened. They have opposed the expansion of airports at Lake Powell, the blading of peripheral roads, the paving of peripheral roads that have been bladed. Above all, they are trying to pass, in the teeth of local politicians, a bill that would protect at least five million acres of canyon country from conscription by industrial society.

It is farcical to read, in the concluding words of the July 1960 *Utah Historical Quarterly*, that Glen Canyon "seems likely to remain a land of space enough, certainly of scenery enough, for all comers for at least a generation." A human generation in the time frame of a canyon wall? It is like using a breath to measure a lifetime. More than a generation has passed since those words were written. If the writer's own children are among the comers, they will hardly find Glen Canyon scenery to come to. It is as if the *Utah Historical Quarterly*, and the economic interests behind it, couldn't wait for Glen Canyon to become history.

Those interests, meanwhile, have given defenders of the remaining canyon country a reliable reservoir of ill will to draw on. It is called Lake Powell.

IV

On October 8, 1992, thirty years into what felt like a canyoneer's afterlife, I continued my lone inspection of the area that had been Glen Canyon. The morning after I located the tiny machine that nattered through the dusk near our push-off point at Hite, I showed up at the ferry that shuttled vehicles across the midpoint of the lake from Hall's Crossing to Bullfrog Marina. It was here that Aspenite Ken Ward had drowned without a trace in the mid-seventies. My immediate interest, however, was in comparing the ferry with Woody's original, his one-car shelf rigged with old mining cable and an engine from a truck.

I pulled into an orderly line of four-wheelers from the Moab Jeep Club and drove as hand-signaled from the boat ramp onto a barge that was three cars wide and five deep. Assorted motorcycles filled in the empty spaces. Some passengers stayed in their jeeps glued to their tape decks, a few wandered the deck with coffee in thermos cups, and some of us watched, surreptitiously, a motorcycle couple going through their yoga asanas. The man had a beard, ponytail, earrings, and baggy polka dot pants, and proceeded in slow motion, standing for a long while on one leg and holding his free ankle above his navel as the craft vibrated its bass note beneath him. The woman, more conservative in beige warm-ups, placed her hands on a cleat for coiling rope and tilted forward until her legs and torso were outstretched in a tense, gymnastic horizontal. The three generations of a family in the station wagon next to them gaped and eyed each other with glee. When he of the clown pants stood straight, stretched his arms skyward, and let out a lone, universe-embracing whoop, the entire station wagon burst into laughter he pretended not to hear. No one, myself included, much looked at the canyon walls, shorn of their height, distanced by the lake. We were glad to drive off the ferry fifteen minutes later and resume command of our own wheels.

I stayed at the wheel all day, pulling by late afternoon into Wahweap Lodge, where I had booked an off-season package tour that included a two-night stay and an all-day boat tour to Rainbow Bridge. From the motel and airstrip where we had ended our trip three decades back, Wahweap had inflated into a resort empire that passed from Art Greene to the Del Webb Corporation, and now to something called ARA Leisure Services. As I made wrong turns through side roads and parking lots, trying to locate the check-in point, I kept visualizing an encounter with Art Greene's family. Katie had kept up with the Greenes over the years. Once during the mid-seventies when she and I were hiking side canyons on the North Rim of the Grand Canyon, we stopped at Cliff Dwellers Lodge, a splendid stone building north of Marble Canyon that Greene had built largely for his descendants. Two of those descendants sat together in the kitchen. The man was barely able to speak because two strangers off the highway had robbed the motel, beating him up even though he offered no resistance. The woman recounted the assault while the man sat before us trying occasionally to interject something, his face nearly paralyzed, his eyes involuntarily filling with tears. I can't remember a more heartbreaking visit with people I only met once. Knowing that Art Greene had founded Wahweap, as well as Cliff Dwellers Lodge, as a commercial venture for his family, all I could see was that stricken face as I circled looking for a parking spot.

The "key" to Wahweap's room 772 turned out to be a plastic card that slid into a slot, changing a tiny light from red to green. The first thing I noticed on inspecting the quarters was that the toilet paper—which we occasionally forgot entirely on desert trips because it can neither be worn nor eaten—had been folded into an arrow. There was a theft-proof hair dryer and a balcony overlooking Lake Powell. As I nursed a beer and watched the sunset bloody Gunsight Butte, I heard an invisible man say to an invisible woman on the balcony beneath mine, "Connie, will you make me a promise that you'll come back here with me in twenty-five years?"

The next morning, with thirty-nine other passengers and two guides, I boarded the *Rainbow Trail* for the all-day boat trip. There seemed a perverse symmetry in taking a memorial tour to Rainbow Bridge, the one spot we had chosen not to visit in 1962 and the one well-known Glen Canyon formation that still stood. The tour barge offered seats for half the party on the unshaded chairs of the upper deck and accommodation for all the passengers below, where windows could be closed against bad weather. All except two young German men, two older German women, and a Japanese couple with a small child were older Americans. I was the only touring American male not wearing a ball cap. As the engine revved, a voice boomed through the PA system, "I'm Lyle and, like it or not, I'm your guide."

Lyle, at the ship's wheel, was a short, fiftyish man in a plastic cowboy hat, wraparound mirror sunglasses, short-sleeved shirt with naval epaulets, and khaki shorts. I had expected to chat with fellow passengers, but the drone of the engine and Lyle made it possible to hear only the trio in front of me, and their tongue was Japanese. As we passed the massive marina, Lyle said, "There's 777 slips here and the waiting list is measured in years." When we cleared the Wahweap complex, I saw a bus cruising midair along a canyon wall and realized that the road, built along one stratum, was invisible from beneath.

Lyle was brimming with information. "Three million people visit Lake Powell every year. The lake is 186 miles long and has just under 2,000 miles of shoreline because of all the side canyons. That's more than our whole Pacific coast from Canada to Mexico. Think of Lake Powell as a giant holding tank. Today the bathtub ring is 78 feet high. That means the lake is 78 feet lower than it was, full, in 1982. The ring is sodium silicate, which some people call alkali." The complex textures, gradations, and stains were sheered at the high-water mark, beneath which all was unvarying whitewash. The Jewel of the Colorado, as the Bureau of Reclamation called the lake in its brochures, may have been star sapphire in the middle, but at the edge it was decidedly paste.

Lyle, it turned out, loved to ask questions. "Does anyone know what those columns are?" he asked, scanning us through his mirror shades. They were, I knew, the three smokestacks of the Navajo Power Plant, winking their strobes day and night so they wouldn't be hit by planes. They had recently been ordered to reduce emissions and stop filling the Grand Canyon with smog. "Those are the stacks of a plant which burns coal brought here by train from the Hopi Reservation. Its connection with Lake Powell is that the water is used for cooling. After that, it's purified and waters the Page golf course," he added with what sounded like a duffer's pride.

More questions followed. "That dark stuff on the walls

above the bathtub ring is called desert varnish. Does anyone
know what it is? Wahweap was founded by Art Greene. Does
anyone know who he was?" There was no way to answer his
questions over the combustion, even if someone had wanted
to. I stared as blankly as the others, comparing his answers
to ones I would have offered. I found it particularly curious
that Lyle spoke of the canyons "running out of water" in the
same way that we speak of canyons "hitting the lake," meaning, from opposite perspectives, that here the canyons end.
We passed a side canyon and Lyle said, "That's Dungeon
Canyon, very popular with houseboats." I gaped, remembering that this was the cleft that reminded me of a late English
gothic cathedral, which pinched to a mad slant thinner than
the human body. Above that slant, apparently, was a useful
lagoon.

After the third fact-filled hour, Lyle was out of material,
and he resorted to finding animal and human figures in the
rocks and folds of canyon walls "to speed the trip"—a candid
admission that Lake Powell might get, well, boring. "I always
thought that rock on the left looked like a seal, but a lady
told me that seals don't have tails that curl up, so I call it The
Chipmunk. That's Dinah, the dinosaur. That's the rhinocer-
ous family. That's E. T. There's The Priest and The Indian
Maiden. Every desert has a camel, and that's ours over there.
That's Snoopy." What, I wondered, would he have made of
Elephant Ass Rock? But as someone who would rather see
rock as mere rock, I avoided Lyle's discoveries and watched
Lake Powell drift through the distortions of his mirror sunglasses. "Know why they call that one Whiskey Cave?" Lyle
looked around as if still expecting answers. "It's not because
anyone stored whiskey there, or drank it—it's because it has
such a hangover." At last the passengers broke their silence
with a well-coordinated groan.

While there was no predicting a guide like Lyle, I had
armed myself with a book I had found in the Wahweap Lodge

gift shop, *Ghosts of Glen Canyon*, by C. Gregory Crampton. I had first read Crampton in the *Utah Historical Quarterly* I had taken on the river, finding his chapter on Anglo history in the Glen one of the valuable contributions. From his later books I picked up what I knew of Anasazi culture. Here, then, was a guide to the lake, with capsule histories of what visitors floated over. But whether the historical feature was a panel of Anasazi pictographs, a mining dredge, a pioneer's orchard, or a river runner's hermitage, all that marked it was one more convergence of water and sandstone at the bathtub ring. All connection between place and event was severed; all history's particulars lay in a common grave. What most struck me was the key word in the book's title: ghosts. Here was the very image that threaded Katie's songs and that sprang from the stories the Glen generated. It was as if everything that happened in Glen Canyon aspired to the condition of elegy and saw its future as a haunting.

Apparently mine wasn't the only mind drifting, for suddenly I heard Lyle saying, "I've learned one thing in my six years on Lake Powell. Want to know what it is?" He looked in vain for someone to ask. "It's that you can't hear someone else when you're talking yourself. Every trip, someone will ask what I just said because they were talking themselves when I said it. I tell them, 'I just told you.' Asking someone to repeat because you weren't listening is not what I would call polite. Now if you don't want my commentary, just say so, because I can also shut up." Fortunately I was just reading, not attempting to talk, but it was a lecture I hadn't heard since grade school, and it was not what I would call polite.

None too soon the *Rainbow Trail* turned into Aztec Canyon, which led, in turn, to our destination in Bridge Canyon. "Only 140,000 people a year see Rainbow Bridge," said Lyle, "and that's not much, considering the population of Earth. Think of yourselves as pioneers." It was a relief to step off the boat onto a marina, then onto a series of planks, then a paved trail over gumbo left by the lake's high level in 1983. The drowned area had been colonized by Russian thistle, which thrives on disturbed ground. It was a further relief to emerge on a path, albeit well-trodden, that threaded yucca, ephedra, datura, squawbush, single-leaf ash, a path that was bristling, diverse, and normal.

Dead ahead was the formation we had come to see, whose surprise value had long been preempted by folders, posters, postcards, book covers, and any number of reproductions. In my own case, I was further jaded from having seen dozens of arches in the thirty years since floating the Glen, and I was delighted that Rainbow Bridge *was*, despite all, grand. Rather than pouring from one high wall to the ground, it soared from both sides, a more improbable trick for stone, giving it the look of premeditated sculpture—which is to say that it looked as man-made as it looked natural. Also, it vaulted over a stream that made it technically a bridge rather than an arch, augmenting its sense of height. When I reached it, stood in its shadow, and looked up, I had a sense that I had recently experienced something like it, something I couldn't place. I was able to stare almost straight at the sun, and the fleecy clouds near it were blinding to someone who doesn't wear sunglasses. Then it struck me that the elusive event was the solar eclipse I had seen south of La Paz, in Baja California Sur, only fifteen months before. There was, of course, no eerie silvering of the surrounding world; it was merely that our source of light was blocked by stone in the sky. The sun, high-flying sandstone, and I were in alignment.

Once I had absorbed the bridge, I saw Bridge Canyon veering off toward Navajo Mountain and had to control an urge to wander upstream, to follow one turn after another, to ditch Lyle and the boat. The only fellow passengers who also went past the bridge were the four Germans and the three Japanese. The Japanese asked me to take a picture of them with their camera. Time was running out, and I returned to the bridge in time to hear a woman from our party remark, "It's just like the arch in St. Louis—when you're underneath it, you can't see anything." It was time to return to our box lunches. When the Germans and I boarded, Lyle said to his assistant, "Good, they're all here. We can go."

From Aztec Canyon we continued farther north, for we were to be shown Anasazi Canyon as a bonus. Anasazi was a favorite of Lyle's, mainly, it turned out, because it was hardly wider than the boat itself. All passengers climbed to the top deck for the cruise's most intimate experience. It was indeed surreal to breach a tight space in a wide craft, nearly able to touch the walls. But what we were face-to-face with, in fact, was the bathtub ring. The sterility, even after a walk we shared with 140,000 people a year, was stark. Not even Russian thistle gained a purchase here; this water and stone was the surrealism of an institutional hall. "Look ahead at those reflections," said Lyle, and they were truly seamless. "After our boat passes, it takes over an hour to get them back." Lyle and his assistant bantered in mock alarm over the PA system that there was no turnaround, but we reached, inevitably, the pool where the boat could rotate, and we unthreaded the white corridor. The passengers had no way of knowing that Anasazi Canyon had once sustained more life than the Rainbow Trail.

The day's sights had all been seen, but the run back stretched several more hours. The assistant took the wheel with a patter more bland, less grating than Lyle's. Then Lyle returned. When we passed the rock that was either a seal or a chipmunk, he said, "I used to think that looked like a seal, but a Danish lady told me it looked more like the Little Maiden of Copenhagen. I never *do* get the seal of approval." This time nobody even groaned; they were too busy exchanging sections of *USA Today*.

Monotonous as the day had become, water and stone in combination are always beautiful, and there is no denying Lake Powell that beauty. It even has a specialty the river's vegetation largely prevented: when sun strikes water beneath an overhang, it sends rippled reflections against the dark stone in bands that create luminous visual music. Those who never witnessed the grandeur of the Glen Canyon cliffs are properly impressed by the red icing that surrounds the lake. But by the elimination of vegetation and the life it supports; by replacing with still water the sinewed, silty, pungent currents that shifted and veered; by truncating cliffs, then cutting their desert varnish with a band of alkali, Glen Canyon has been simplified to the point that it can't hold the attention. Three million people a year go to Lake Powell, but they go to Lake Powell the same way that they go to the beach. The lake is a venue—for fishing, waterskiing, partying—and a venue is a place waiting for something else to happen. Suddenly Lyle was saying, "We call that formation the Winnebago."

I looked to the rim and there, salvaging the afternoon, was a trailer-shaped rock, complete with cab, in perfect parody. This country looked forward to more than elegies after all. It had seen us coming.

v

Katie Lee, for all her hatred of Lake Powell, once remarked that if it hadn't drowned, it would have been trampled to death by the hordes that have descended upon the Grand Canyon and the better known surviving canyons in Utah. It is certain that, like the Grand Canyon, it would have to be rationed, with the inevitable battle for permits between commercial outfitters and those out for a private float. Canyons that narrow to the width of a person cannot entertain like reservoirs.

But even as a reservoir nearly two hundred miles long, Lake Powell is in trouble. Scientists researching Lake Powell for federal agencies have found that lake sediments contain twice the normal concentrations of chromium, copper, magnesium, and zinc. Mercury levels in fish have reached four times the level considered safe for human consumption; selenium has accumulated in some fish in amounts to cause their reproductive failure. Culprits in these concentrations include naturally occurring erosion from the basin's formations of Mancos shale, along with runoff from farming, grazing, and mining. Visitors, meanwhile, add their own contamination. In the summer of 1992, eight beaches were closed and swimmers were warned away because of colliform bacteria, caused by boaters emptying toilets directly into the lake or onto nearby shores. Park officials may soon supply the lake with floating waste disposal systems. Even those who come to Lake Powell to fish, water ski and party may find their health in jeopardy, their activities curtailed.

Unbelievably to those with long memories, obliterating, ruinous Lake Powell manages to be loved by some with a passion like that once kindled by Glen Canyon. Most poignant is the story of a couple from Littleton, Colorado—he, twenty-nine, she, thirty-four—who had AIDS. They shot their Rottweiller and then themselves on the shore of Lake Powell and were found by two little tourist girls on November 13, 1992. They left a careful suicide note in the room they had rented at Bullfrog Marina Lodge, saying that of all the landscapes available to them for their last sight of earth, they chose Lake Powell for its beauty.

In another generation or two, no one alive will have a personal memory of Glen Canyon. The once pulsing lifeline at the heart of the canyon country, its dim and soaring side canyons, its native American ruins and pungent shores will exist only in books, photographs, and journals, phantasmal as Troy or the passenger pigeon. The remains of Glen Canyon lie under what is quite literally a winding sheet of water. To abolish a landscape is not merely to destroy; it is to engage in collective amnesia. It becomes incumbent upon us to keep Glen Canyon alive if only as a wound that will not heal, to give us eyes and hearts, the precedent and the rage to defend what is left.

One Step Beyond

Simply by being assigned a date and a theme, our national
holidays are more focused than the days that surround them.
Three of us—Karen, the caretaker, and Remo and I, the guests
—converged for Thanksgiving at a ranch amid the swirling
sandstone of southeastern Utah, twenty miles from any neighbors. When Karen bought a turkey of wild stock in the nearest
town, she also learned the route into a canyon none of us had
explored. The day before Thanksgiving we defeathered the
bird and scouted the route, preparing our scenario: first the
canyon, then the feast. Thanksgiving would be pale and brief,
but full.

Despite our preparations, we squandered Thanksgiving
morning on extracting the last pinfeathers and stuffing and
trussing the turkey so that it could cook while we were off
exploring. We had five hours of daylight left by the time we
bundled ourselves and Karen's shepherd mix, Koa, into her
battered station wagon and bounced to the canyon rim. Gaz-

ing from a prominence near our descent, we marveled that a formation as dense as stacked plates allowed human passage. Koa, sweet-faced and stoic, rode in Remo's arms as we scrambled down a break in the top layers. When we reached the crucial traverse, Karen said, "Koa, pay attention." We crawled along an indentation two feet high and just wide enough to cradle our pounding hearts. A boulder plugged its exit. To make ourselves thin, we held our daypacks in outstretched hands and rolled over the rock's top, inches from the ceiling. Koa crawled after us, graceful and self-possessed. Soon we were down a talus slope and into the main drainage.

After such serious preliminaries, we felt liberated from common sense as soon as we reached the bottom. We lingered by an Anasazi petroglyph, joking that the bent comet shape next to the schematic man would encourage speculation that the Ancient Ones were contacted by visitors from space. We crawled into free-standing perforated rocks that wrapped themselves around us like wishbones and femurs from O'Keeffe. Adult enough to lecture a dog, we were like children in Grimm, frolicking as darkness encroached.

Given scant time and a prankish descent, we should have gone back the way we came. Karen's informant in town, however, had mentioned that we could climb out on a cow trail in a side canyon two miles downstream. We would certainly see more by making a loop, and the two miles to retrace would be on top, after all, on the flat. As we forged foolishly downstream, the sun was nearing the canyon rim. We had a single flashlight and no sleeping bags. Thanksgiving was a month from the winter solstice. In return for bilking this American holiday, I saw us missing the cow trail, divining our tracks back in the lone beam, fumbling for the rock that stoppered the crawl between stacked plates, or, more likely, cuddling with Koa to pass a polar night. We were courting what is known, in the West, as a situation.

The side canyon appeared on cue, sheer, gently curving out of sight. We saw no break in its walls, bovine or otherwise, but it kept veering, withholding its end. Remo thought he saw a way out and scrambled toward what looked like a barricade near the rim. Karen and I continued to the end of the canyon. At its last recess, a spill of rubble climbed partway up. Through the binoculars I traced an improbable line of brush that crossed rockface, rubble to rim—nothing I would call a cow trail but perhaps the way out. As dusk thickened, we waited for three whoops from Remo, a signal that meant, "Come, I've found something." Eventually Remo appeared in person, panting, saying his route wouldn't make it. We stood while he caught his breath.

It is unusual to hear any erosion in that land of stone, so slowly does it crumble by human standards, but suddenly, across our side canyon, rock exploded. In that grasp of threat that is quicker than thought, we knew we were personally out of harm, but the next split second burned itself through our eyes and into permanent consciousness. In the midst of a spray of stone from a three-hundred-foot cliff hung a stag deer, its antlers outspread, its legs moving faintly, suspended for a fleet, interminable second. With an echoless whomp it was on the ground, a shadowy, formless heap across the drainage.

We stood in stupefaction. The bulk was twitching, then still, with a back leg distended at an irrational angle. Karen burst into tears. Koa stared blankly. I raised the binoculars. We stood mesmerized, then each of us repeated what we saw, to make sure we saw the same thing. We gazed at the cliff for an explanation. It stared back blankly, so sheer that the deer could only have fallen from the rim. Karen remarked it was too bad we couldn't pack out the meat. Now we wanted daylight to piece the event together—to reach the animal, count antler points, and learn its age; to work our way to where stone and deer sheered off; to determine the cause. As it was, we would be lucky simply to get out of the canyon and find the car.

A path switchbacked through the piled rubble, then reached the line of brush. The vegetation turned out to be dried sticks woven at the brim of a natural ledge, mere psychological fortification that was propped, at the scrawniest point, by a tree trunk poised on a rock. It was inconceivable that anyone had maneuvered a cow this way for years, and the vision of the plunging stag made all mammals newly vulnerable. Oddly, we were less concerned for ourselves than for Koa: how could we still trust surefooted nature? Koa took the purported cow trail with aplomb, scampering above and below as fragrance called, and we all reached the rim intact in the last light. Remo's reckoning and flashlight and Karen's knack for picking her way by starlight had us back to the car in little over an hour. A Thanksgiving we thought was going to reward our foolishness with chilled marrows offered, instead, the most riddling moment any of us had known in the wild.

Seated, at last, in front of our overcooked turkey, we asked each other what the day had meant. It is always unsettling to catch nature making a mistake, and it seemed doubly suspicious, in that unvisited country, to arrive at just the instant when a huge, precision creature, honed by the millennia, made a fatal misstep. We ruled out coincidence. We were, we decided, unwittingly to blame: the deer heard voices below, stole to the edge to look, and went down with an unstable formation.

We had set up this day—first the canyon, then the feast— as an empty frame to step into, and the frame now held something inscrutable. We had remarked that Thanksgiving was a favorite holiday because it celebrated gratitude rather than, say, patriotism or theology. But what did a deer falling from the sky say about gratitude? It showed, if anything, its compromising nature. A stag's demise was Thanksgiving for the coyotes; a spectacle of mortality had strangely exhilarated us. Eating our ceremonial meal beyond reach of electricity, sipping wine by candlelight removed from others of our kind, we were graced with irreducible experience. Reasons to give thanks are traditionally one step beyond comprehension.

Transition Zone

As pavement climbs north from Phoenix, the expanse of cactus fractures like a shook jigsaw. Smooth desert suddenly rears into domes, palisades, crenellations and rockfalls, labyrinthine, crazed, a troll's nightmare. The phenomenon is known as exfoliation, literally, the losing of leaves. The substance is granite that cracks at roughly right angles. Once it has been cubed, the corners crumble faster than the faces, a geological way of rounding the square. What the square loses on the way to circlehood is what becomes desert sand. Solid granite? The desert's mother lode is sheer rot, rock on its way to becoming a million square miles of kitty litter.

The whole formation registers a bare mile on the odometer, two drainages splintered by assorted cracked ribs. I had driven through once too often, and one January afternoon, on a whim, I pulled off below and stopped to explore. That two-hour ramble took on the contour of an allegory.

Hiking up the first ridge and gazing into the stratum, I was struck by a 180-degree sweep of flesh-colored jumble, a single organism becoming many. Beehive formations barely held together; broken columns leaned against each other for support; boulders sprawled with no plan. Rain that had slid from the rocks filled pockets between them with sharp green—paloverdes, jojoba, and, because this was the topmost rung of the Upper Sonoran, the leathery beginnings of chaparral. This softening was punctuated by vegetation that seemed firmer than the rock itself, the shafts of great saguaros. A formation splintering apart, sending up numberless green lives—it was what theologians might call creation by division.

I made my way to the smooth sand at the drainage bottom, then started into the rocky panorama. There was no way to pick a route beforehand; one could only clamber from rock to rock, calculating two or three boulders ahead. The coarse granite easily held my boot treads, but granules pulverized into sand even as I climbed. My arms—atrophied as the arms of most hikers—got a workout as I hoisted myself through this stone jungle gym. Often boulders were too big, defied passage, and I had to descend here and try over there. Or I was funneled into vegetation between the rocks, where the serrated edges of barberry leaves and the spikes of yucca waited on point. Backtracking, zigzagging, I won my way to the next ridge, across a small drainage and onto the spine of the formation. The foreground of intricate granite suddenly gave way to vast distance. Low clouds hung over peaks luminous with fresh snow; far darkening relieved busy foreground. As I caught my breath, a clatter burst beneath me, and I spun in time to watch a four-point stag bound through the very rocks I'd been threading. I followed the ridge in a kind of exaltation, watching the stone labyrinth fall beneath me as hanging clouds heightened the far mountains. I came to a virtually boulder-free fold that escorted me back to the main drainage, over the ridge, and I was back to the car in two hours. As I say, the ramble was like an allegory, though fortunately there was no one around to tell me what it meant.

Once I had sampled the place on foot, I made time for exploration every time I passed. I hiked it from the top down as well as from the bottom up, at different times of day. I became familiar with topography that always sprang surprises. I saw clumps of hedgehog cactus whose tips had been eaten by javalinas, the pulp gone, the spines and skin strewn like fast-food wrappers. A saguaro had a wraparound lower limb like a skater descending into a sit spin. There were cardinals, the relatively uncommon ladderback woodpecker, and one day I flushed a great horned owl. After a February storm I came upon a free-standing granite basin cupping melted snow, so symmetrical it could have been commissioned with tax dollars. I sat and drank: the water was cool, bland, sublime.

Sated with rocks, I became aware of the way moss and grasses filled their hollows, particularly on north slopes, and the way lichen covered the rocks themselves. Growth-coated rocks weren't flesh-colored at all; they were olive, baize, mustard, day-glo chartreuse, and, more interestingly, a perfectly unreflective, eye-resistant, matte black—one or more of the 120 species of Andreaea, commonly known as granite moss. Here and there were bright green shotgun shells and sometimes I heard shots, for no desert seems complete these days without the most dangerous predator. My winter explorations were well timed to avoid the second most dangerous predator, the rattlesnake, which is really only dangerous when it can't see you coming: in places like this. As the season warmed, only the open sand in the central wash would be secure from snakes, and I had already walked its length, back to the highway and underneath. The culvert was a cold plunge where dry air suddenly hung dank, my footsteps rang from all directions, and pupils tightened by bright granite were unmoored by concentric rings where corrugated iron caught the far sky.

Most of all, I liked to sit on the first ridge as day declined and rocks leapt forward as individuals from their shadows. I could rehearse the way granite cooled and hardened from magma beneath the surface. Tectonic forces lifted it, exposed it, relieved it of subterranean pressure. It cracked along perpendicular faults. The outer surface of the rock dried rapidly after rain and snow, but moisture that seeped inside was caught until decay set in. Layers peeled off in the unsheathing of exfoliation, also known as spalling and spheroidal weathering. Lichen, the first plant to colonize land, clung to the layers as they fell, perhaps even helped them go. Here, in this vegetal transition zone, where cactus mingled with chaparral, was a geological transition zone, rock released into sand. Just as a spring is a source for water, so is disbanded rock, for a desert, pure source.

Staring until I had only enough dusk to find my way out, I liked to imagine the whole formation disintegrating under the moon, in darkness, offering new soil at first light. No other corner I know of so merits some lines I remember from Robinson Jeffers:

> *I have seen the dust on a summer day*
> *Crying to be born as much as flesh*
> *Ever cried to be quiet.*

Cactus Pete

When I read that the Magellan Orbiter had sent back infrared photos confirming that mountains on Venus were higher than those on earth, I hopped in my van and drove south of the little town of Florence, Arizona, to ask my friend Cactus Pete whether he felt vindicated. I had to wait for his coughing fit to stop.

"I was merely thirty years ahead of them," he snapped in his quick, rasping voice. "Back in 1962 I read that some scientists in Tucson were making a geophysical map of Venus. That's just when Kennedy wanted all that money to go to the moon. I took my own map of Venus and asked to compare it with theirs. They laughed and said, 'You show mountains.' I said, 'That's because there *is* mountains.' These guys all had billy-goat whiskers, you know, very important. I thanked them for their time and left. Now they're spending more millions to prove what I've already got. I don't even know where I put Venus. It's rolled up around here somewhere." The years had not unscrambled Pete's brain, and I was glad to find him still alive.

Pete had been a loose thread in my life since the early seventies, when I first explored Arizona as an adult. In the course of trying every road in the state, I took the old highway between Phoenix and Tucson. Interstate 10 siphoned off traffic, turning the former artery into a country lane where mallow blooming in every conceivable shade crowded the shoulders. South of Florence, as fields gave way to saguaros, I came upon a knot of buildings blistering behind a wall. A small water tower under wooden scaffolding hung over saguaros dense enough to suggest a cactus garden. A sign said Rancho Soledad—Ranch of Solitude—and didn't indicate whether it was public or private. As I pulled in, jackrabbits zigzagged in front of my car, the sun shining through their ears. A family of quail wound its way into the underbrush, orioles flashed from the paloverdes, doves exploded in all directions. I felt I had burst into a wildlife sanctuary.

I parked and looked for someone to tell me to leave. There was no one to tell me anything. I proceeded between a pair of long, low buildings with evenly spaced doors that suggested living units. Between them cracked a pool filled with bougainvillea leaves. Random small buildings sprawled to the side, their cement blocks painted to resemble adobe. Agave, barrel cactus, ocotillo, aloe vera, cholla, and prickly pear, including strains from other locales, were clustered with a density nature reserves for rain forests. Around me chattered finches, woodpeckers, quail, thrashers, and cactus wrens. Toward the north, where I had come from, the profile of the Superstition Mountains suggested the Super Chief, the train that my father—already retired when I was growing up—took downtown three days a week as a "consulting associate." Brimming with associations, Rancho Soledad looked as if someone had tried to reduce the whole Sonoran Desert, with parts of other deserts, into a single garden. My heart was beating wildly: would it be possible, somehow, to *move into* this place?

As speculation ran wild, I found myself being stared at by an old man who had emerged from behind my car. His mouth was a ruled line. Slight, bespectacled, pencil and Kleenex stuck in his pocket, jeans rolled over his boots, he looked like a professor gone to seed. Not knowing what to say, I blurted, "Are there any rooms for rent?"

"You kidding? This place isn't open to the public anymore." I realized there were no teeth to give his mouth definition.

"OK if I look around?"

"Suit yourself. I'll show you what there is." The place had been built in the thirties as an obscure spa for Easterners bitten by the desert. It had changed hands a number of times. Parts had remained rentable to various degrees, other parts disintegrated. Its future was even more obscure than its past, for it was now owned by an elderly woman in Minnesota who was in the care of nurses and—the old man was sure—of law-yers who were conniving to take the place away from her. She had asked him to caretake the place. More as a favor than for money, he had done so for a number of years.

While he didn't encourage conversation, neither did he fend it off, and I asked how he had wound up here. "From Philadelphia. I had scar tissue in my lung and was given a year and a half to live. That was in 1928. I came to Phoenix and ran into a salesman who was traveling the state. He took me through here, said, 'This is a nice area, Pete. Why don't you homestead it?' I said, 'I think I will.' I went back to Phoenix and took out papers. I made up my mind I was going to get better or the hell with it. I'm sixty-eight years old and I'm still here."

Years of sun and the loss of teeth made Pete look older than he was, but the story of Easterners who were given up for dead, moved to Arizona, and lived to extreme old age was a familiar one: my father made the attempt. Already sixty when I was born, on his second marriage, he had smoked Lucky Strikes almost since they hit the market. To grow up was to watch the deterioration of my father's lungs. Winters in suburban Chicago left him gasping. Because he was retired, because I was young, and mostly because rules were looser, my parents simply pulled me out of school for months at a time and we headed south—directly, or by Southwest—looking for air to breathe. Cigarettes, not climate, were my father's unraveling, and because he smoked wherever we went, every haven was a mirage. My mother caught our passage in watercolor and I saw the world. And the best of the world I saw was thirty miles northwest of Rancho Soledad.

In the late forties and early fifties, the air around Phoenix was still pure enough that doctors were telling pulmonary patients to go there rather than to stay away, and many others at the dude ranch had breathing problems. People who coughed like my father were called "Arizona canaries." While my father worked crossword puzzles by the pool, smoked, and attempted to breathe, and my mother was wielding her paint brushes and golf clubs, I discovered the desert. In Illinois, birds built nests; here they gouged holes in pillars of pulp called saguaros. The ears of rabbits were so thin you could see light through fur and flesh. Families of quail wound through the shrubbery like electric trains, lizards vanished into crevices, and roadrunners' legs were as blurred as hummingbirds' wings. And after it rained, the pungency of the creosote bush stirred your lungs with an ache to be just where you were.

I was often the only child on the premises, but there was nothing stern about adult life that revolved around horseback rides, chuck wagon dinners, square dancing, costume parties concocted by a social hostess, drives on the Apache Trail, and shopping expeditions to Nogales. Adobe cottages around patios were filled with people who stayed weeks, or months, and became family. A seasoned hotel brat, I played the piano in the lobby, won at bingo, and beat businessmen at gin rummy. Wanting desperately for my mother to share the desert, I lured her up Camelback Mountain, where we got trapped over a drop-off. My adventure was her trauma, and after that she seldom ventured beyond sight of her clubs or her easel. One morning all guests were told to report to the pool at eleven for an important surprise. We arrived to find that bathing beauties of a sort never before seen at mature Jokake Inn had been placed in strategic positions. Photographers shot the aquatic mob scene from every angle, and the next September we received an *Arizona Highways* with the three of us on the inside cover—my father working a crossword in a formal gray suit, my mother in a two-piece bathing suit, my pallor stretched on a pad—swamped by glamorous extras. Desert dude life was fulfillment: why bother with anything else?

Time, as I later learned, cures paradise, and when I got to high school, my parents were not allowed to pull me out for a ten-week stretch. My father ultimately went cold turkey on tobacco, but the damage was done and he didn't live to see my college graduation. My mother married another Arizona-bound Chicagoan and wound up living—as if coached by her paints—only a few miles from where we had first seen the desert. I visited a couple of times over Christmas, then spent a season with a friend near downtown Phoenix. When my mother was widowed a second time, I simply moved in with her every winter. Perhaps the creosote had chafed my lungs the way tobacco had my father's, for the desert had become my addiction.

Phoenix, however, was overcoming the desert. The so-called bedroom community where my mother lived became a corridor community, as if it had been kicked into the hall. Winter temperature inversions trapped the particulates, blurring and sometimes annihilating the horizon. Spores from introduced plants gave people lung problems they didn't arrive with, and Arizona canaries were told to try one of the smaller towns, maybe Prescott or Wickenberg to the north. Camelback Mountain bristled with electroguarded homes, and the homespun Jokake Inn had been replaced by a five-star Xanadu pitched by the eminent swindler, Charles Keating. Reaching the desert meant threading a battlefield of streets ripped up for widening, sewer lines being trenched, vegetation being bulldozed, and phone, power, and TV cables being slung or buried to service bermed layouts of townhouses, villas, and ranchettes among groundwater lagoons. Slowed but unstopped, I fought my way through to the cacti. And one day I drove past a sign that said Rancho Soledad, straight into my childhood.

Since there was no way to move in, let alone to make a rash offer to buy it, there was nothing left but to drop in now and then, to stroll through the delapidation, and to talk, increasingly, with the opinionated Pete. "The city fathers of Florence didn't know what they were doing. They tore down a bunch of old territorial buildings because they were ashamed of them, when they could have restored them and turned Florence into another Santa Fe. That Senator McFarland was the crookedest politican we ever had. The interstate should have come through here, but McFarland bought land outside of Casa Grande, got the highway to go through there, and made his bundle. So what does Florence do? It turns the old hospital into a historical museum and names it for McFarland. That's Florence City Hall for you."

When Pete didn't show up at the eroding spa, I tracked him to his ramshackle house to the south. The old lady in Minnesota hung on from year to year, attended by nurses, plotted against by lawyers. At last she died, but the estate was in probate and the fate of Rancho Soledad became no clearer.

After paying my respects to the ranch and to Pete, I usually completed the visit by eating in the restaurant just to the south of Pete's house, a place with its own peculiarities. There was nothing odd in its desperate swing between cheap steaks and Mexican fare, a pattern for marginal restaurants all over the West. Its rambling, low-ceilinged rooms were classically road-house, but the building's south end, over the bar, was a half-cylinder like a tin can split lengthwise and placed round-side up, its rondure sagging in parody of a covered wagon. Beyond the cylinder, at the acute angle formed by the highway and a back road to the cotton farming town of Coolidge, stood a free-standing white tower of four cubes, each smaller than the one beneath it, exaggerating its modest height. Door locked, lower windows boarded, upper windows giving on darkness, it was a Babel for sparrows. Between this assortment and the road, visible for miles either way, stood a pair of date palms like spiky feather dusters. The whole line-up—from Rancho Soledad through Pete's house, the restaurant, and palms to the tower—mutated from nostalgia to dementia. This, it seemed to say, is what can happen to civilization in the desert.

While Rancho Soledad was in probate, I was browsing the southwestern section of a used bookstore in Santa Fe and was caught, as if by a saguaro spine, by the spine of a book that read *Cactus Forest*, by Zephine Humphrey. No mention of Rancho Soledad appeared on the jacket, but I was so sure the place lurked inside that I paid $7.50 for what was marked as a "First Edition" even though I suspected it was the only edition, and whisked it to my motel room.

The tale, published in 1938, begins in Vermont, where the author's husband is laid up with sciatica and all remedies fail until the sixth doctor commands: "Arizona. Lie in that dry sunlight all winter and keep away from doctors." On their drive West, a waiter in Lordsburg, New Mexico, informs them that he too had sciatica and wasn't cured until he went East. Tucson, where they plan to settle, is abrasive and full of tourists. They head north over roads I had explored in my Arizona wanderings, until they find just what they're looking for "five miles below Florence"—the precise location of Rancho Soledad.

Congratulating myself on my intuition, I next read that they settle into an adobe cottage made by "a young Philadelphian who, eight years before, had gone to Arizona for his health," and whose name is Erwin Peters. I knew from Pete's mailbox that his name, officially, was E. A. Peters, assumed his nickname came from his last name, and that "Cactus" was added by Florence neighbors. Erwin, therefore, was the young Cactus Pete, and his place was something called Cactus Forest Ranch—a half-dozen one-room housekeeping cottages hidden from each other in the desert. Forsaking her usual humor and invoking the sublimity used to embalm Frank Lloyd Wright, Humphrey says of the place: "Never was variety more skillfully employed to embroider unity; never did unity more serenely triumph over variety, using it for purposes of complete integrity." The Humphreys watch Erwin wrestle with burst plumbing, and a fellow guest helps Erwin build a new cottage. Erwin's mother, embarrassed by her German accent, presides over the Peters living room, a gathering place for guests. The image of restored health, Erwin treats himself with an undisclosed kind of "animal oil," as well as a "mineral mud" from "elsewhere in Arizona." One morning, as if to prove a point, Erwin appears at the Humphrey door "coughing and wheezing," tells them a cold is no problem, and returns from Coolidge at four that afternoon "completely cured by one chiropractic treatment." The Humphreys had always scorned chiropractic, but after hearing Erwin rave about the Coolidge chiropractor, Christopher Humphrey goes to a Phoenix osteopath recommended by a friend in Vermont. The osteopath evens Christopher's legs, he lies in the desert sun, and halfway through their stay he steps out of his sciatica "as if it had been an old pair of slippers."

Cactus Forest Ranch? And no mention of Rancho Soledad?

The next time I dropped in on Pete I was full of questions, and I asked him about the book.

"Zephine? Oh, yeah, nice lady. Came here several winters. She signed a copy to me. I've got it somewhere with my maps. I've just mapped Jupiter. Know that red spot? Turns out to be a premonitory."

I didn't understand a thing after the part about Zephine and was determined to pursue the matter of the cottages. "Pete, what's Cactus Forest Ranch?"

"That's a few guest places I built across the road. It was sometime in the thirties. Lots of the guests were millionaires from the East. They told me they liked it better than being at home, that it was really living. There was an aide to General Pershing who stayed with his bodyguard. Also that guy Juilliard who built the music school in New York. His wife was always worried about his hump. They weren't all rich." Zephine had mentioned an archaeologist, a woman who broke her writer's block and finished a book in two months, a pair of businesswomen, and a rodeo rider. "I also put up a six-room adobe house for ourselves. My mother came out and stayed awhile. They put manure instead of straw in the adobe, the termites in the manure ate all the woodwork, and we had to pull the house down. The cottages fell down on their own. Know that black hole they found? There's interesting minerals on it."

What I really wanted to pursue was why Zephine hadn't mentioned Rancho Soledad, since it would seem to have been there at the time, and she even mentioned (misspelling it) Jokake Inn, forty miles away. But I could see Pete's mind was elsewhere, so I said, "Do you have some kind of telescope?"

"Don't need one. I've mapped all the planets. There's mountains on Venus but nobody will believe me. I'm part of the Earth's surface. I do it by magnetism. If it wasn't for magnetism, nobody'd be alive."

"You mean you just draw the surface of the planets free-hand? You don't use an instrument at all?"

"I use my doodlebug."

"Your which?"

"Gizmo I made myself. I'll show it to you sometime."

Sometime was not now, and I left finding the little string of buildings more cryptic than ever.

When the will was settled, the resort didn't wind up in the hands of lawyers, but it was uncertain whether it would be offered for sale or bought by the county for a rest home. On the possibility that it might actually come on the market, I asked Pete to take me inside the buildings. The largest of them, where the owner had lived and provided a common room for guests, would have made a perfect desert home by itself, and I was particularly impressed by some hand-carved doors I was unaware of. There was a root cellar I'd never noticed, a gap in the weeds that proved to be a shuffleboard court, and Pete pointed out an organ pipe cactus from Peru. More eye-catching, alas, were the crumbling guest quarters surrounding a cracked, empty pool. The water table had dropped and the well had to be drilled another twenty-five feet. The plumbing and wiring were shot and had to be redone. Looking at the matter coldly, I could see I was trying to recapture my grade-school idyll under Camelback Mountain. The reality was that patching, buttressing, supervising, and restoring would be thrust upon someone who really didn't like to handle anything messier than a dictionary. You couldn't be a hotel brat and also run the hotel.

I had by no means abandoned the area and had developed a fondness for Florence itself, an unassuming town with a couple of good Mexican restaurants and a tiny downtown that got a minor tidying for a minor film with James Garner and Sally Field called *Murphy's Romance*. While its surviving territorial buildings were on the National Register, its most appealing structure was an eclectic 1891 brick courthouse with mansard roof, dormers, and circular windows. Zephine, who had higher standards, called it "a sheer architectural monstrosity." Because there was no money to buy a clock for the polygonal cupola, dials had been painted in all four directions, reading seventeen minutes to twelve. There was something winsome about a town where it was always quarter-to-lunch. In the notion that Florence might not be a bad place to live outside of, I dropped into a real estate agency, explaining that I was interested in living in unpopulated desert—did they have anything to show me? "Hop in," said a realtor who had just arrived from a boom in Alaska.

We cruised in his sedan past Rancho Soledad, south toward Tucson. "What do you see as the future of Florence?" I asked.

"Frustrating. The whole town is owned by a couple of families who don't want the place to grow. The State Pen is the only real business here, and the people who run it don't even live in Florence because there's no place for them. They commute from Mesa, Phoenix, even Tucson. We'd like to get a Safeway, but a chain won't come unless there's a certain number of people, and we're below the minimum. These families own all the little businesses, and they don't want the competition."

We pulled onto a dirt road, bottomed out in some potholes, and crossed a cattle guard. "What I'm showing you is a strip of private land that just came on the market. It's got BLM land front and back, so you'd never have any neighbors except on the side, and these are five-acre parcels. They're prime and they'll be going fast." We walked several of them; cactus soared, paloverdes hummed with bees, and house finches chattered excitedly. Realtor's hype aside, these lots deserved to go fast. But if I didn't want to patch, how could I conceive of contructing? Scavenger that I am, I was looking for the perfect shell to fill like a hermit crab.

On the ride back, the salesman, thinking he might have put

me off with the backwardness of Florence, said, "Well, even if the town doesn't want to improve, we could still get the world's largest jetport."

"The *what?*"

"The aviation facilities in Phoenix and Tucson are both too small, and this would be something really future-oriented, right in the middle."

"Isn't it a little far from each place?"

"They're talking light rail in both directions, but the airport wouldn't just be for passengers. Federal Express is very interested. This could be the shipping hub for the *whole Southwest.*"

We rode the rest of the way in silence. I took the realtor's card, then drove back fast to Rancho Soledad. "Do you know anything about a plan to put a jetport in Florence?" I asked Pete.

"Sure," he said, his cavernous mouth beaming for the first time. "Been talking about it for years. This time we might actually get it."

"Where would it be in relation to Rancho Soledad?"

"We're standing on it."

"Wouldn't you lose everything here?"

"Lose? Think what I could leave my kids!"

Around this time, two Florence-related incidents pursued me to Phoenix. One was that Pete and I had adjacent letters in *The Arizona Republic.* Mine protested the overcutting of forests; Pete's promoted the jetport. Since Pete never actually learned my name, only I could relish the irony.

The other incident involved a pre-concert drink with a friend my concert-mate wanted me to meet. For some reason the conversation turned to Florence. "It's a wonderful place," said the friend's friend.

"Really?" I asked eagerly. "I'm thinking of buying some land there and possibly building."

"If you do," he said, "I'll have to give you a letter of introduction to a friend of mine there, William Weaver, the opera commentator, who also translates Italo Calvino. He's got a villa and is surrounded by servants. He's terrifically bright and great fun."

How odd that someone so sophisticated as William Weaver should live in Florence! Still, with interesting company added to cactus and Mexican food, perhaps I should make use of that realtor's card. . . . About halfway through the concert, as the Phoenix Symphony was sawing through some Schumann, it suddenly burst into my head that all through the conversation my friend's friend was talking about Florence, *Italy*, while I, monomaniacally, was talking about Florence, Arizona.

Having floated Glen Canyon just before it was dammed, driven the Baja Peninsula before the road was paved, lived on Cannery Row before it became a boutique, and in Aspen before it appeared in the *National Enquirer*, was I now about to put down roots in Florence before the jetport? For someone whose sense of identity derived from surroundings rather than a nuclear family, emotional survival was increasingly a lesson in nonattachment, and on learning of the jetport, my interest in Florence, as the locus of my future, crested and waned. I let years pass between visits. Did Rancho Soledad go through a rest home phase? I got little information from Pete. "I don't think it's working out for the county. There's a few people there paying rent, but I don't have to mess with it anymore. These big outfits make me mad. I just wrote to the School of Health at New York University. I told them I'd like to get some blood samples of AIDS. I think I've got the answer. They said the government wouldn't let them ship anything like that. Instead, they sent me a report this thick. I threw it in the fire."

While I no longer thought of becoming Pete's neighbor, the inscrutibility of his corner picked at me. It seems I'd over-reacted to the specter of the jetport, for the Phoenix papers never mentioned it until a politician, fishing for rural votes, resurrected it in a speech and prompted an editorial in the usually development-minded *Arizona Republic*, saying they assumed that particular imbecility had been laid to rest. Less momentous questions still nagged: how did a desert home-steader map the planets? What was the significance of the square tower? What was the cure for AIDS? On reading that the space probe had discovered mountains on Venus of the sort Pete had mapped in his back room, I drove to Florence in a mood for answers. After a three-year absence that would depend, of course, on finding Pete still alive.

I pulled into Rancho Soledad, past a For Sale sign. A man in his sixties was sitting on the porch of one of the smaller buildings. "Is Pete here?" I asked.

"Who?"

"Cactus Pete. Erwin A. Peters."

"Oh, sure. He's living across the road, in the house under the water tower."

I now knew there were two water towers in the neighbor-hood, as well as the restaurant tower. Pete's current house was as ramshackle as the other but set back from the high-way, more private. I called "Pete!" let myself in the gate, and knocked at the door. Soon there was Pete peering through the screen, the sky behind my head glittering in his glasses. "Yeah?"

I explained that I saw that NASA had confirmed what he'd said about the mountains on Venus, had been interested in various things he'd told me over the years, and would like to ask a few questions if that was all right.

"Sure, come in." He held the door open. "Do I know you? You have to excuse me. I've had a few strokes."

"I'm the guy who kept asking about Rancho Soledad."

"Oh, yeah," he said, though I wasn't sure he made the con-nection, anymore than I'd ever been convinced that he re-membered me from visit to visit. He'd looked older than his age when I first met him but hadn't changed much since and now merely looked his age. "Sit down. If you'd come five minutes earlier, you'd have missed me. Just came back from the chiropractor in Coolidge. Just got over a cold, but I can't seem to shake this cough. Mountains on Venus?" He dissolved into a spasm of coughing and wheezing that ended in gasps for breath. As he told me how he'd first mapped the Venusian ranges back in 1962, I stifled the urge to ask if he'd just seen the same Coolidge chiropractor who had cured his cold in 1937, as reported by Zephine Humphrey. I could see that he was more bent than before, and though the day seemed warm to me, he was bundled in a shapeless sweater leaching some shade of faded.

"If this isn't a good time, . . ." I began.

"Let me make a fire." He stooped to a pile of sticks, laid them in an iron stove angled in the corner, and lit them.

"What kind of wood is that?"

"Just dead creosote, OK for some quick heat. I get it with a wheelbarrow. When you're eighty-six, you gotta keep busy with something. I found out how to take the radiation out of those power lines, to make them safe. I wrote and told them, but they didn't even answer. They'd rather take government money to bury the lines, which won't solve the problem. At least I got a letter back from Mrs. Bush, so I'm that far ahead."

I was always impressed that Pete, unknown and marooned in the desert, never shrank from the world's stage. Since he had plunged in, I didn't hesitate. "How do you get out the radiation? The same way you map the planets?"

"With the doodlebug."

"Can I *see* the doodlebug?"

"Haven't I ever shown it to you?" He seemed genuinely surprised and headed to the back room. In his hand when he returned was a small spring with a rubber handle on one end and a plastic cone on the other. "Hold your hand out." The doodlebug wagged puppyishly in front of me, seemingly impelled by a motion in his wrist. "You're full of nuclear, but I've taken the nuclear out of that chair. Sit down." I sank into a gray armchair with a towel draped over the back. "Now get up." He held the doodlebug in front of me. It was as still as his wrist. "See? The nuclear's gone that quick. Let's sit down."

After we settled, I said, "I still don't understand how the doodlebug works."

"I got a bunch of them. They're easy to make. All you need is a spring and some uranium."

"That's what's in the tip? Uranium ore?"

"Exactly. Uranium ore."

"So the force is atomic?"

"No, it's magnetic. Way I figure, I'm in the negative return circuit. I pick the magnetism up through the doodlebug when it comes back from the sun. Your college boys won't recognize me because I'm not one of them. I had two-and-a-half years of high school."

"How did you get the idea to do this?"

"Mining. I mapped mining properties. If I wanted to find a mineral, I'd make a map, then go pick the mineral up. I made the first doodlebug fifty years ago. That's how I got onto planets, doing mining."

"Is it like dowsing?"

"Sort of. The doodlebug finds things underground. I started a vertical map of this place years ago. The ocean's been in here seventeen times. I dug a hole and put a pair of crossbeams on each level, to show where the oceans were, but when I was almost finished some kids pulled the cord and they all came out. Kids are terrible. But when you correlate the seventeen oceans with the oil, it fits. Some of the cactus around here look like coral, and I know the sea is where the desert plants come from."

I remembered that the desert reminded Frank Lloyd Wright of the ocean partly because the staghorn cactus suggested coral, but what was metaphor for Wright was evolutionary evidence for Pete. "So you struck oil?" I said.

"I found oil just across the road, 800 feet down. A guy from Coolidge raised the money to drill from a company back in Massachusetts. My boy and I worked on that well for nine months, and as soon as we hit oil the company shut it off. They wouldn't pay me for it, and we didn't have the money to work it ourselves. The mining companies only want your information. They tell you they're not interested, then they move in after you've gone. I wouldn't let them do that to me, so all I've got are some samples. I'll get one."

I was grateful for a moment to collect stray thoughts and inspect Pete's living quarters. The furniture was like Pete's sweater, faded and shapeless, with towels over the backs of chairs and a blanket over the sofa. Taped to the wall were pictures of children, a portrait of Barry Goldwater, and clippings about solar energy and Arizona political scandals. Across two walls was a collage of objects, mostly iron, arrayed with an eye to design: horseshoes, spikes, canteens, ice tongs, a mining pan, ax blades, and, wired to the wall, a green bottle whose red label rebounded from pre-Jokake childhood. I jumped up to make sure, and there was the red devil prancing in front of a massive hotel. It was Pluto Water from French Lick, Indiana, where my parents took me when I was seven, when my father could still breathe. We had stayed in a grandiose resort built around a spring that smelled like rotten eggs and was bottled, my mother said, "for people who can't go to the bathroom." I was reading the fine print on the label, lost in the nostalgia of first travel, when Pete reappeared with a half-gallon jar. "It's Pennsylvania oil, but we hit it in water." Oil and water oozed in layers in a way that reminded me of lava lites, lamps of gaudy, heated, writhing liquids people stared at in the sixties—nostalgia of later travel. "All the oil around here is mixed with water."

"If this area has so much oil, why didn't the big companies ever come in?"

"Phillips drilled an exploration well down the road in Tom Mix Wash, and Mobil drilled further on, but they didn't do it right. Hell, I could have told them, but they didn't ask me. There's surface oil right on the property."

"Can I see it?"

"Come on." We proceeded outside, and Pete deposited the oil sample on a table where another two dozen jars stood like sun tea. He grabbed two plastic cups, and we passed through old stoves and tires into the cacti. "This stuff belonged to my partner. He died awhile back. Isn't this air wonderful?"

The air was soft and delicious. "Pete, has the desert changed much since you got here?"

"There's a lot less growing now. See how there's no little plants?" It was true; the bursage, brittlebush, and varied grasses were missing; between the saguaro and barrel cacti was packed, bare earth. "The county made a diversion in a wash a couple of miles from here and never figured where the water would wind up. Every time it rains, the water floods through my property and washes away the topsoil." It suddenly struck me how much Pete *did* make sense: the predation of mining companies and the ignorance of the county were perfectly plausible. At this point I spotted some black lumps on the ground ahead and thought, "Surely not." To my stupefaction, Pete bent down and peeled off what I recognized as black cryptogamic, a lichen and algae community that holds the desert soil in place. He handed it to me and said, "What did I tell you? Oil, right on the surface! Look at it." I held it close and saw the tiny plants, like hairs of black velvet. Before I could think of what to say, he put the cryptogamic in one of the plastic cups and said, "Come, I'll give you more proof. I've also got paraffin."

"Wax?"

"Wax, whatever. It's associated with oil." We started back

toward the house. He set down the cup of cryptogamic and descended with the other cup into a tight arroyo, raising his arms away from some catclaw acacia. The Superstition Mountains, floating over his head through the cacti, seemed aptly named. He bent down and picked some moss off one bank. He started to climb out, slipped, grabbed a creosote branch, and pulled himself back up. "You get this old, you lose your balance," he grumbled.

We continued toward the house and suddenly he stopped, breathing hard. "I feel knocked out," he gasped. "I shouldn't exercise after a cold. There's probably an earthquake going on somewhere. No matter where in the world it hits, I feel it. You'll probably read about it in the next couple of days."

He breathed easier and returned through the gate. He set the plastic cups on the table and said, "Let's check these out. If it's oil, it should fizz." He opened an unmarked brown bottle, the fumes reached him before he could pour, and he began to choke. When his breath steadied he filled each cup.

"What's the liquid?" I asked.

"Hydrochloric acid." Each cup looked full of mud and neither fizzed. "Maybe it will take awhile," he said. "Let's go in and sit down."

I was relieved he had survived our excursion and felt the need to change the subject. "Pete, did you build Rancho Soledad?"

"No, somebody else built that after I got here."

"Zephine didn't mention it." Pete had arrived in 1928, eight years before Zephine arrived with her sciatic husband; either she had written around it or Rancho Soledad was built after 1936.

"I can't remember now what happened when, but I homesteaded 640 acres and built a lot of other stuff, like the Chuck Wagon Restaurant and that tower."

I had struck oil. "What was that tower for?"

"It was to advertise my gas station. Saguaro Petroleum was

the Gulf agent in Phoenix and they said, 'Peters, we like your location.' I said, 'What does that do for me?' They said, 'If we can put in a 5,000 gallon tank, we'll give you a 9 percent margin.' I had a windmill on the corner, but who looks at a windmill? I took off the blades and the tail, encased the rest in plaster, and painted it white. The Saguaro Petroleum people outlined the whole thing in red and green neon. By the time it was finished, you could see the thing for fifteen or twenty miles either way. It was about the *only* thing you could see."

I had pictured the tower's four cubes deliberately shrinking on the way up to make it look taller. "You mean there's a windmill inside that tower still? Why is it built to look like four boxes?"

Pete looked surprised. "A windmill slants toward the top. If you're going to make a tower, you've got to square it off."

"Did you let people go in?"

"I never fixed it up on the inside or let anyone in for fear there'd be an accident. It was just for show. The only person but me who went up it was a convict who escaped from the pen in Florence. He stopped for water at the well at Rancho Soledad, was about to be caught, broke into the tower, climbed up, and begged for mercy out of the top window."

"And the round part of the restaurant, next to the tower, was meant to look like a chuck wagon?"

"Originally it was the *whole* restaurant. It doesn't look like a chuck wagon now because some people I sold it to added all that square stuff that's much bigger. I made the wagon by bending reinforcing rods at different radiuses, stretching chicken wire over the rods, then pouring plaster over the chicken wire. The quonset hut came out soon after I opened the restaurant, and I think that's where they got the idea. My best customers weren't from the road. They were those rich people from the East I rented cottages to. They liked nothing better than to go across the road and have breakfast in their pajamas and bathrobes—it was something they couldn't do at home. They loved it. You were looking at that bottle a little while ago, that Pluto Water."

I didn't know I'd been caught. "When I was little, my parents took me where that stuff comes from."

"That was my novelty drink. I gave it away free, and also to minors who wanted alcohol. One kid got mad because he lost his girlfriend when she got diarrhea. The Chuck Wagon lost him his date, but it got me my wife. The superintendent of the hospital in Florence came in one night with two nurses. I saw one of them and said, 'That's it!' I married her. We had a pretty good life together. Then she broke her back. That's when I started the clinic."

"Besides the cottages and restaurant and gas station, you had a clinic?"

"The clinic is the only reason I ever wanted money. A long time ago I was looking for perlite with a partner out of Superior, and he told me his wife had breast cancer. After we found the perlite with the doodlebug, I asked if I could use the doodlebug to take the cancer out of his wife. In ninety days I had her in remission."

"I don't see the connection."

"Magnetic. Same as I took the nuclear out of you when you sat in my chair this morning. So when my wife broke her back, and was gradually paralyzed, I set up a clinic in the back of the Wagon Wheel, complete with two osteopaths, phones, and equipment. I taught them what I knew about magnetic and nuclear. They both made enough to move out on me. They took everything I gave them, even the X-ray lab. My wife died after that. That's when I made my mind up that anything I tried to do, I had to do on my own. So before I kick the bucket, the one thing I want to do is get a clinic going."

"A *new* clinic?" Sometimes I found myself repeating to make sure I'd heard right.

"There's a doctor now in Tucson who brings patients to me when he can't do anything for them. I take the radiation out of them so they have a chance to get well. When people get sick, I get answers. They gave $5 million in New York for a report saying that everyone exposed to power lines was going to die from cancer. Hell, I've got the cure, but they're educated and won't listen to someone like me. And they won't send the AIDS blood. So you see the politics."

"And after your wife died," I said, returning to an easier thread, "you never remarried?"

"Not actually. When my partner died, he left a nice little woman. When I was driving back from Wyoming once, something told me to drop in on her in Glendale, outside of Phoenix. I had a feeling. She came to the door and said, 'Oh, Pete, you're just in time. Take me to Florence.' I said, 'Get your duds together,' and she lived with me for ten years. Never had an argument, never got married, had a good life together, then *she* got sick. I used to put out feed for the quail, and she'd sit all day watching them. So I outlived her too."

The idiosyncrasy, the complication, the withstanding of loss in this scrap of American road culture brought my thinking to a halt. To get started again, I summed, "Besides Rancho Soledad, which wasn't yours, there was the restaurant, the gas station, the clinic, the rental cottages, the house with the manure, the tower around the windmill . . ."

"And the amusement park. We had a merry-go-round and a train. It was the adults who really loved to ride the train, especially after a few drinks. I built it for my son. There was a fight in the school bus and he got hit on the head with a book. It knocked him out for a long time and I was afraid of brain damage. I wanted to leave something to support him if he couldn't work. But he turned out OK, and I closed the amusement park the day we took in seventy-five cents. I also have two daughters, and they're OK, too. A lot can happen in sixty-three years."

"Whatever happened, this had to be the biggest thing on the road between Phoenix and Tucson."

"Road?" Pete laughed. "There was no road when I got here, just a dirt track, a so-called military highway from 1889. I worked eighteen years just to get it oiled and the town of Florence wouldn't help me. That's how progressive they are. Everything I ever wanted, Florence was against. I had the Mexicans on my side, and the truck drivers wanted the road through Florence, but Florence was run by the Presbyterian church." Perhaps he was overcome by the notion of Presbyterians, for suddenly he began to cough uncontrollably, ending in spasms and gasps.

"If the doodlebug can cure cancer and AIDS," I ventured, "can't it do something about that cough?"

"What?"

"Can't the Coolidge chiropractor cure your cough? Or the doodlebug?"

"These colds just go around. Everybody gets them."

While he recovered his breath, I sat, further digesting information. Pete didn't mind the silence, for unless pressed he didn't speak at all. Now and then thoughts demanded to get out, but there was no urgency to voice the transitions. "Pete," I finally said, "where do all your ideas come from?"

"I take a shot of Jim Beam whiskey every night before I go to bed, with some water and sugar so I don't get too much booze. But that's to *stop* thinking. Some nights I can't sleep at all. Things come to me and I get up and work them out. When Mount St. Helens erupted, I put it on paper. I located those missiles in Cuba. Remember those H-bombs that were missing off the coast of Spain? I wrote the Air Force where they were. What's the name of that colored general?"

"Colin Powell."

"Powell. I sent him a map of Hussein's headquarters, not that they'll give it to him. That's why I wrote to Mrs. Bush. I said, I know your husband is too busy with the Persian Gulf deal so I'm writing to you. I also wanted President Bush to know I had the answer to the power lines."

"The radiation?"

"Yeah. To prove to Mrs. Bush that I knew what I was talking about, I sent her a diagram of an atom. It's radium, carbon—Christ, I can't think. I've had some seizures. Anyway the power companies were on NBC a couple of weeks ago, trying to get the President's OK to move or bury all those lines so they won't cause cancer. Of course they want the government contracts. I could go to each plant and show them what to do instead. There's 112 companies, and I want $45,000 from each one. That's $5 million."

Suddenly I felt as if I had fit together two remote pieces of a jigsaw. "Isn't 5 million the amount you said you needed to build a new clinic?"

"That's the one thing I want to do before I die, the one thing I want money for. I can cure people, and I need to pass that on. Let's look at those specimens and see if they've fizzed yet."

The afternoon sun hit us square in the eyes. The mud in the two plastic cups had partially settled, green shading to orange at the top in a way that suggested tomatillo sauce going bad. "See?" he said simply. "It's oil."

It was clearly time to leave, but I had to satisfy one more bit of curiosity. "You know, Pete," I said. "I've never actually seen one of your maps. Could I see Venus?"

"No, you can't see Venus because I don't know where I've put it. It's the first one I did, and it's way back somewhere. I'll show you something else." We went back to the house, into a small room with a workbench smothered in tools. On the floor, so thick we could barely stand, were supermarket bags filled with large rolls of paper. He pulled a roll out of a bag at random, took it into the living room, and started unfurling it. I took the end and held it until seven feet of paper, three feet wide, stretched with vibrant color between us. "What is it?" I asked.

"Halley's Comet."

Shaped vaguely like a map of Malaya, it was a ragged-edged, intricate mosaic of meshed polygons shaded with colored pencil—a Balkanized, tutti-frutti, hundred-faceted gem cut by a jeweler gone mad. Black lines that burst into wire stars stuck out like spikes from the perimeter. I asked to see more, and Pete showed me two: Uranus and an object called Levy's Comet—named, he said, for a Tucson astronomer who discovered it but wouldn't look at his map. Assuming that the grocery bags held roll after roll of such creations, here was a major collection of original, baroque, beautiful, unwitting folk art. In the guise of a crackpot scientist, here, perhaps, was the Grandma Moses of American abstraction. The sheer complication and scope were impressive. "How do you do it?"

"With the doodlebug. The doodlebug moves around, and wherever it moves I make a line. I just think of some celestial object, put the paper on the workbench, and start."

I couldn't picture doing such intricate and precise work with the gizmo in one hand, and I realized one would have to watch to understand. "What are these spidery lines on the outside?"

"I think they're collectors that absorb the radiation that gives these objects the power to turn."

"Both these comets are angular. I thought comets were round, with tails."

"This is the way they came out. In all the articles they write, comets are ice and goo. But look at all these colors. Every color represents a different mineral. And these are only the important ones. I didn't put in the iron and stuff."

At the top of Halley's Comet was careful writing, upside down. "What does that say?" I asked.

"It's a list of the minerals that correspond to the colors. I've written it upside down so it's harder for people to read if I show it to them, but I'll let you look."

I turned the paper around and read, out loud, "Radium, uranium, mercury, iridium. *Caliche?*"

"That's calcium deposit."

I knew very well what caliche was. Caliche, alias hardpan, was that unyielding layer under the Sonoran desert that scorned anyone trying to install basements or palm trees. Caliche was that saline, calcified flooring left when lakebeds dried, that mineralized solution that rose from the subsoil through capillary action, to congeal where the hot, ravening air couldn't reach. An inch thick or a yard, it informed anyone who pried beneath that the desert's granular surface is a false bottom. By extension—and what were Pete's maps but extension—caliche was the impenetrable layer of politics, betrayal, survival of loved ones, failure to be taken seriously. Caliche was the Florence Presbyterians and caliche was what filled my father's lungs. Pete had been resisting caliche ever since the doctors gave him a year and a half to live in 1928. Anyone could work down to caliche, but it took a desiccated, sand-blown, persecuted, calloused, moonstruck desert rat to find caliche on a comet.

Wigwam for One

When it takes over four decades to satisfy a wish, chances
are that by the time the wish is satisfied, the wisher will have
changed. In 1950, when my parents drove from Chicago to
Phoenix on Route 66, my rabid, fiery, implacable desire was
to stay in a motel room shaped like a wigwam. My parents refused to patronize roadside trash despite my tantrum. It wasn't
until late in 1992 that I pulled up to the Wigwam Motel in Holbrook, Arizona, a collection of cone-shaped units surrounding a gravel courtyard. Both my parents were gone, Route 66
had been supplanted by Interstate 40, and a kid's frustrated
adventure had turned into an adult encounter with restored
highway schlock. Perhaps my parents were still with me, for
I felt them shudder when I entered the office and asked for a
wigwam for one.

As I approached my white dunce cap with its tiny diamond-
shaped windows, its door framed by plaster folded back like
cloth, its red zigzag trim, I wondered chiefly whether the room

would be round or square and whether the ceiling would rise to a point. The shock was complexity. A straight wall near the back of the room, hiding the bathroom, paralleled the wall with the door. Negotiating the perimeter between them on each side were four smaller walls that met at wide angles, completing a ten-sided room. At shoulder height, each wall angled inward toward the ceiling, creating a space like the crown of a brilliant cut diamond. I sank in a hickory and wicker armchair to admire this faceted embrace, and flicked on the floor lamp next to me, eight hickory sticks leaning inward in parody of the wigwam itself, capped by a red lampshade like a fez. White walls, hickory desk and bed frame, curtains and spread with the same black and red design—except for the TV and the air conditioner that plugged one of the diamond windows, it was all of a piece.

It was a very strange piece, however, and once I had absorbed it, I returned to the office for a chat with the owner, a laconic man named Chester Lewis II. In 1948 his father, Chester Lewis I, saw a wigwam motel in Orlando, Florida, and decided it was just the thing for Route 66 in Holbrook. He used the same design, did much of the construction himself, and opened it in 1950. The architect, one Wally Redford, allowed seven motels across the country to be built from his plans, asking only that he be allowed to outfit each unit with a radio that played a half-hour for ten cents. His architect's commission was collected monthly out of the radios, in dimes.

Holbrook's Wigwam Motel was an immediate success, and even became a traffic hazard when cross-country gapers braked and got rear-ended by locals. In 1974 came the Interstate, bypassing Holbrook, and the motel closed. During the thirteen years that the wigwams stood empty, Chester Lewis I died and the cult of Route 66 bloomed. In 1987 Chester Lewis II opened a restored Wigwam Motel, complete with its original hickory and wicker furniture from Bedford, Indiana. The rooms, says Lewis, are packed in the summer and busy the rest of the year. I wondered a bit at commercial wigwams on the edge of the Navajo Nation where the indigenous house is the low, dome-shaped hogan: what did Native Americans think of the motel? "I have Hopi friends who call all the time for reservations," said Lewis. "The native Hopi building is the pueblo, but they tell me they love these wigwams."

When I returned to my own wigwam, I saw that I had left the door open and the lamp on. The fez beckoned through the folded doorway like a hearth fire. Because each unit stood alone, there was no aural bleed-through of TVs and no pipes that sang when the neighbors took showers. But because I had requested a unit in the back, away from the business route, I was closer to the unseen railroad tracks behind the motel, and the peace was assailed each time a freight lumbered symphonically through Holbrook, trembling the bed, rattling the grill on the heater. I heard, sharped and then flatted by the Doppler effect, the minor triads of the engines' horns while the metal wheels crackled on the gaps between rails. A way of life, perhaps passing, was at the moment passing right through me. On a bed become a berth, I thought of all the old jazz songs based on trains, realized that it wasn't just the romance of a machine aimed at the horizon, but that the wailing horns and syncopation of the rails *made* a kind of jazz.

Between trains, my mind played riffs on the roadside wigwam. Wasn't the wigwam actually a small structure of saplings and woven reeds, made by tribes of the Northeast? Surely this schematic shuttlecock more resembled bison hide stretched over poles, created by the Plains Indians and known as a tepee. But this design, pitched by Anglos to lure compatriots who didn't know one tribe from another, was Fantasy Indian, not Native American. Since Hopis were amused, perhaps they would lend a word for the style. I dropped off mulling the term *kitschina*.

When I checked out in the morning, I asked Chester Lewis II who the most frequent customers were. "More than anything else, we get people who stopped here with their parents when they were kids, and for them it's nostalgia." I didn't tell him that in my case, despite an impressive tantrum, it was nostalgia for what I had missed.

The Floating Observer

The shift in perspective begins at lift-off. The palms around the airport, the houses among oleanders could be features in an herbarium. Mountains that imposed a presence through the windows, even as the plane taxied, take on the anonymity of waves as the horizon leaps beyond them, revealing farther mountains—wave upon wave. Between them, toothpick saguaros soften the valleys, shrubs and trees condense around the watercourses, arroyos contract like waterlogged skin. Roads slash at random, a madman's attack. Over this cryptic surface, clouds add their own layer of abstraction, dragging their shadows over vegetation and geology in unrelated pools of darkness.

It is disconcerting to look out of a plane window at a familiar landscape. The earth's skin has become as detached as a slide under a microscope, its elements tiny, oddly shaped, alien to ourselves. Yet there we live, lost among them. The dislocation may be purely visual, but amidst the hum of the engines, the rush of cool, metallic air, and the chatter of passengers, sight is the only sense still related to the landscape at all. In this reduced atmosphere, with the other senses at bay, eyes work overtime, tracing how mountains drown in their own runoff, how towns metastasize from the highways, how deltas fan into the sea. The view from above is informative, but the knowledge gained is structural, cerebral, shorn of contact.

At cruising altitude, then, what cruising *attitude*? Partly, it is an awareness that the landscapes that engulf us can be reduced to design. On the ground, for instance, it is difficult to believe the assertion of astronomers that the earth is exceptionally smooth for a planet; that Mars, smaller than the earth, has higher mountains and deeper canyons; that our blue ball has been worked by water until it has become, for its size, smoother than an orange. At cruising altitude the astronomer turns out to be right, and it is only the infinitesimal specks of ourselves, ants on the lawn, who contrive to make things huge. Gazing down from 30,000 feet, it seems doubtful that any god who created all this could care, individually, for his creatures.

The overview does have its compensations. Flying directly over a mountain range whose folds are obscure from the ground, you can see the whole pattern laid out—how the valleys run, where the vegetation indicates water, which is the highest peak. If you scan fast you can decide whether an area warrants exploration by foot, even plan your next trip. But to look down on a mountain range you love is perhaps to know too much. A sprawling, intricate structure lies open to inspection, dismaying in its finitude, seemingly stripped of its hideouts. Dead of overexposure is the mystery that bloomed from its base. You master the range's countours with your excitement on hold. You must take for granted, as an act of pure faith, that emotions will flood back when you next confront the mountain on your own two feet, armed with news from the heights.

Along with the aerial decoupling of landscape and emotion comes evidence of another decoupling below. Roads cut like swords through geological knots. Irrigated rectangles plaster the desert with iron-on patches. Pit mines inscribe plantar warts in the mountainsides while cities, under palls, square off the valleys. The straight line, the circle, the acute angle, the grid—these Euclidian staples overlay the former grain of the land, which shows through in the dimmest pentimento. The organizing demon you have recognized in your own mind, peering through a small window and reducing the world to pattern, is busy below with compass and T-square, straightening, leveling, rounding off, turning that pattern into simplicity you can't care for. If you still feel an emotion up here in this pressurized tube, it is fear that the very genius that holds you aloft is pruning the world of every treasured eccentricity. On some future flight you may descend to a world for which, on the ground as well, you can feel nothing.

What a few people feel or don't feel during flight time may be of little consequence except as a curiosity. The distance reverberates only because we seem to be withdrawing farther and farther from the earth right on the ground. As with movies, television, fast surface travel, even the written word, the remote overview is one more wrenched perspective that developing civilization has glued, collagelike, to the once unified experience of life. The view from a plane is especially hard to absorb, being the ultimate experience of nature as remote and glassed out. Superficially, the airline passenger is like the scientist poring over a Landsat photo, tracing the vegetational and mineral patterns of the earth's surface, wielding a detective's eye. But the scientist, trying to understand a structure, exploit a resource, or salvage an ecosystem, concentrates his whole awareness on the earth's structures, and its surface remains charged with meaning. The flyer, flung between two points on a flattened globe, may find that all connections have snapped.

If the airline passenger is a figure for technological man, the rule seems to be that the higher we fly, the less we feel. On or off a plane, if we are to live deeply in a world fractured by media, human manipulation, and the rapid transformations of space, we will have to live like the Landsat scientist. If we are reduced to our eyes, sight itself must swell with feeling. Fascination with the world will have to substitute—briefly—for immersion. At cruising altitude, that means that life on the ground, petty as it looks, still counts. As the alchemists said, as above, so below; and in the swirl of contemporary experience we will have to become alchemists of a sort, drawing the word, the image, our feeling, and the view into some awkward, wobbling, transitory, private but comprehensible singularity of focus.

For the juggler of experience, it is no doubt exhilarating to gape from a plane window and gain perspective on fond spots below. It is, nonetheless, a relief when wheels again touch tarmac, when mountains impose personalities through the plane window, when the terminal takes scale from tossing palms. It was a mistake to take the overview, to believe one was too slight to matter. The ant's life resumes, charged with significance.

Squeek

Whatever else we may require in the way of water, cacti, cottonwoods, salt flats, or snow, for some of us the landscape isn't complete without an eruption of pianos. Most may be props of bourgeois living rooms, but the best-placed of them are springboards to adventure. The sight of an unplayed upright made in Chicago, where I, too, was made, once impelled me to join an Andalusian band in a Spanish nightclub, leading to a string of gigs in an unplanned three-year stopover. Returning to my adopted town of Aspen, Colorado, I snooped its odd corners by playing parties, melodrama, silent movies, and finally classes for the summer camp of Ballet West. Flawed technique frustrated me in the repertoire I preferred, but the ability to remember or fake tunes on demand led past the notes toward experience.

Freelance playing leads toward experience only if you keep moving, and after two summers of chopping all music into the eight, sixteen, and thirty-two bar bites required for dance classes, I was glad to find a replacement in a certain Squeek Moore, friend of a friend, from Philadelphia. "Squeek" seemed a better name for a violinist than a pianist, but when I asked the ballet mistress how Squeek was working out, she replied, "Great. She can fake more music than you can." My real reward for playing for Ballet West, it turned out, was getting to know my successor.

Within two years Squeek had talked a low-budget company into three times my salary, and in the twelve summers she played for Ballet West I watched, impressed, the way she used music as her own springboard to experience. As head of the music program for a Philadelphia high school, she staged such multi-school productions as a kids' musical she wrote, called "Hare," while moonlighting in Philadelphia nightclubs. One year she circled the globe, climbing Kilimanjaro, teaching and making music in Thailand and New Guinea. She lit sometimes at her cabin in Jackson, Wyoming, but there were few pianos in the area besides her own, and the lack of attendant jobs kept her from settling in. When she, too, burned out on chopping music into multiples of eight bars for dance camp in Aspen, I went several years without seeing her. I knew from phone calls that the following sentence about her had appeared in the "Physiology and Anatomy" section of the *1990 Guinness Book of World Records*: "Barbara 'Squeek' Moore performed on the piano from memory 1,852 songs at the Philadelphia Bourse Building from Oct. 25 to Nov. 13, 1988." Also, she had moved to Virginia City, Nevada.

Virginia City? I had never been there, but I knew too well the old mining towns that worked the tourist trade in Colorado and Arizona. Wooden false-front buildings with covered sidewalks were propped back up to house the Bucket of Blood Saloon and Rosy O'Grady's. Bartenders with graying handlebar moustaches wore stained leather vests, and someone at a rinky-tink upright butchered Scott Joplin under a sign that warned customers, ill-advisedly, not to shoot the piano player. In breaks between saloons huddled souvenir shops with T-shirts, ashtrays, mugs, and naughty bumper stickers. Gritty museums drew ore-cart buffs and in the distance rose slag heaps from a now romanticized generation that had gutted and run. Admittedly, my own town of Aspen—an old mining town now catering to the linguine and umpteenth-home crowd—was merely whoring in a different direction, but my usual reaction to towns that recycled the mining motif was to case the souvenir shops, buy anything really offensive, and decamp. When I arrived at midday at Squeek's one-story clapboard Victorian house in Virginia City, the first thing she said was, "I'll tell you about *Guinness* later. First, you have to see downtown."

Squeek, now in her early fifties, lean, with small bright features, was wearing an ankle-length black silk dress with lace trim, fastened with a cameo pin at the neck. Her hair, formerly straight and graying, was now straight and blond. Her companion Roger had gray hair, shoulder-length and curly, complemented by rimless glasses, a gray linen suit, and string tie. In my plaid shirt and cords I felt like a sticky key. We passed false-front wooden buildings with covered sidewalks and parked, just as I had pictured, in front of the Bucket of Blood Saloon.

We also hit the Red Garter Saloon, the Mark Twain Saloon, Solid Muldoon, Calamity Jane's, The Brass Rail, and the Ponderosa Saloon. Most had pianos, and most of the pianos were playable. Squeek played Scott Joplin impeccably and I, as a perverse experiment, played Rachmaninoff. Some bars had pianos with snapped strings and non-functioning pedals, known in the trade as piano-shaped objects. Some had player pianos with built-in drum, cymbals, and xylophone, which we played with coins. A few customers watched, but more hunched over electronic poker games built into the bar. The highlight for me was a piano I'd heard of, designed for Irving

Berlin. Able to play only in the key of C and needing to write in various keys, Berlin commissioned a piano with a lever that shifted the whole keyboard to the right or left so that the keys hit higher or lower strings. The piano company, having spent a great deal to design one instrument, made ten, of which this was a rare survivor. Chopin's "Etude in A Flat" was ravishing in D. Virginia City was just as I had feared but for one factor: I was in piano heaven.

In the late afternoon, when we made our way back to Squeek's, I asked if I could hear the story about *Guinness*. "Later," she said. "First you have to see the house." My eyes had already been touring the living room's odd free-standing chimney, its heavy sofas and oak chairs, and the stern pair of husband-and-wife portraits that Squeek identified as two sets of great-grandparents. "Roger will show you the rest" she said.

We proceeded through a room with electronic equipment into the kitchen, where the sink, with its ribbed porcelain draining board, reminded me of the one my mother was trying to get rid of as I grew up. The bathroom was overwhelmed by a ceiling light fixture with bulbs pointing up and down. Explained Roger, "It was made when electricity was first introduced and people feared it would fail, so the lower bulbs run on electricity and the upper ones on gas. The house was built in 1879, and there are no fixtures more recent than 1939. That's the year that technology peaked in terms of livability."

"Where are you from?" I asked.

"The past."

On our way back to the living room I paused at the electronic keyboard, the computer, the VCR. "This technology looks more recent than 1939," I observed.

Roger smiled, expecting it. "We have to work in the 1990s."

It wasn't until the next morning that Squeek cleared two interrupted hours to tell me the *Guinness* saga. It began with an innocent remark to the drummer who served as her agent, that she thought she could play ten thousand songs from memory and get into the *Guinness Book of World Records* but didn't know how to go about it. Replied friend Rob, "I'll call them. I'll produce you."

There existed no music memory category in *Guinness*, leaving Rob and Squeek to create any format *Guinness* would accept. Rob sent a proposal to *Guinness* headquarters in Enfield, England, and in July 1988 they received approval to try for the book. The only time both of them had free was the following October, leaving Squeek little more than three months to cram.

One might assume that Squeek would prove her memory by sheer length of time played, but she and Rob planned to turn the occasion into a benefit, with individuals pledging an amount for each piece, and the number of pieces made the better fundraiser. The "Minute Waltz" was thus favored over the "Apassionata Sonata." The sponsoring nonprofit was the Gray Panthers, whose founder, Maggie Kuhn, lived in nearby Germantown and would be celebrating her eighty-third birthday during the event. The venue was set for the Bourse, the former Philadelphia financial center—now converted to a shopping mall—next to Independence Hall with its famous cracked, bell-shaped object.

Squeek's greatest problem wasn't summoning the music but remembering which music she knew. Her brain had been involuntarily recording notes since her infancy in Ashland, Kentucky. She could play extensively from memory by the time she started lessons at age eight, and she figured out the oom-chuck oom-chuck of stride bass when she was ten. Studying classical piano and organ at Oberlin Conservatory of Music in Ohio, she realized that certain East Coasters could play circles around her technically but not without the score. She studied and taught in Quebec, Salzburg, and Washington, D.C., before settling in Philadelphia. Trying to retrieve what her mind had stored, Squeek poured names into a tape recorder—kids' songs, pop, Methodist hymns, classical, rock, musical comedy, African folk songs, ballet—a brainscan that took six weeks. Rob arranged the two thousand titles into alphabetical categories for the judges.

Once she had her list, there remained little more than a month to play through the selections. "I memorized by hearing notes, not seeing them, and by then I was nearly fifty. I put a tape recorder on in my mind and just let it soak in. I might not have played a tune since I was seventeen, but it's there if I go through it once. Very often I couldn't remember the middle part and had to recrystallize it. I had this way of squinting and crunching into my hearing certain chord structures. My brain felt totally expanded. I couldn't believe how much I could stuff in. I'd wake up in the night with four different songs going through my head in counterpoint, then think, I've *got* to remember the middle part of 'Once in Awhile.' Of course, you must love on some level what you're memorizing."

While Squeek was squinting and crunching, Rob was lining up judges, sixty-one in all—orchestra and jazz musicians, ministers for hymns, ethnomusicologists for African repertoire, a fiddle-tune specialist, a TV producer, the Philadelphia Director of Housing, a psychiatric nurse who sang gospel, and third graders. Asked to justify the latter, Squeek said, "Only a third grader knows obscure stuff from the third-grade songbook. The youngest was eight years old. They were my toughest judges."

The Bourse, a three-story atrium surrounded by suspended walkways, grillwork, and decorator lights, reminded Squeek of a Paris railroad station. She played five hours daily, midmorning to midafternoon for three weeks. Every time a song was approved, a turning wheel activated a scoreboard with the song and pledge total to date. From two to four judges sat at a table by the wheel, and the Gray Panthers tended a spread of literature. The only competing noise was a popcorn wagon, and the only distractions were from Squeek's interior.

"Every time a piece was called, I'd have a brief flash of the music and whether I knew it. The judges were always switching genres, so I was always changing gears. After I'd finished an Offenbach ballet piece, they'd ask for "Sitting on the Dock of the Bay" and I'd lose the middle. Middle parts are the worst and a few pieces were thrown out because I couldn't remember them. But if I didn't want to postpone a shaky piece, I'd just jump in. I'd fly through the chorus, not having any idea of the middle and not wanting to screech to a halt. It was like careening down a hill toward a gate; in the last beat before the middle the missing information would drop into place, the gate would open, and I'd sail through. It seemed to me a lot of things that happened in my mind had nothing to do with music. My brain felt crammed. Then for an hour afterward each day I'd feel ecstatic, like I'd just climbed Kilimanjaro. I was free of emotional problems and outside stuff, and I felt very *cleansed*. Then I'd go home and go through more music."

So who was watching all this?

"The mall wanted publicity to draw shoppers downtown, and it got them. People who worked downtown came regularly to eat lunch—they could get a sandwich at the Greek place, then come listen. Sometimes they'd request a song, which I would play for three dollars, and it would be one I'd forgotten I knew! That offset some of the ones I knew and forgot. There were old people who said they hadn't heard certain songs since they were kids. My favorite regulars were the bag ladies. One in her late thirties wore the same clothes every day for three weeks and talked to me like an old friend. Another took a photo of me and gave it to me in a plastic key ring, even though she had no money."

Despite the people, did it ever seem to drag on?

"No, because I turned it into a show when I could. I played a six-foot walking piano—a giant keyboard whose keys light up and play when you step on them. It was introduced in the movie *Big*. That gave me exercise and the onlookers visual relief. Rob would bring his drums and sit in. A lot of kids showed up, and I put them to work. When the judges called "Tutti Frutti" I taught them the part that goes "Wop-bop-a-loo-bop-a-wop-bam-boom" and they sang back-up. The Gray Panthers had a birthday party for Maggie Kuhn. A blind saxophone player showed up the last day. I wanted to extend the event, but the Bourse set a limit. Every time the judges asked for "I've Had the Time of My Life," I said I was saving that for the last song. Finally, I had to play it."

How much of the list did she get to?

"It was only two thousand songs long because I didn't have more time to identify what I knew. Ten thousand, in any case, was just a wild guess when the idea was born. Between the numbers I blew, the extras I was requested, and the ones I didn't have time for, the final figure was 1,852. We sent a concluding report to *Guinness*, including the names and credentials of the judges, the times and place, newspaper clippings, videos, T-shirts, buttons, and a judge's initials next to every song I played. It took a month to get the paperwork together and two months for them to reply. The sentence that was the apparent point of the whole thing appeared in the 1990 edition. There's still no guarantee that sentence will be carried from year to year, but the experience of getting it into print was the real point."

And what, I wondered as an awed friend, had led someone who had scaled a musical Kilimanjaro to settle into the seeming lowlands of Virginia City?

"After *Guinness*, I was relaxing at my cabin, and Roger, who lived in Jackson, said I had to experience Nevada. Reno turned out to be boring, but the hotel had a brochure of a Victorian town I'd never heard of, up in the mountains, named Virginia City. The first bar we went into next day looked like it hadn't changed in a hundred years—no plants, no brass, no designer wood like you'd find in Santa Fe or Aspen. There was a piano in back, and I don't go anyplace that has a piano, occupied or not, that I don't ask to play. The bartender said, 'Here's two free drinks.' Next bar had a piano. Here was a town of 700 people and every bar had a piano, with more pianos in hallways, churches, the courthouse, an inordinate number of pianos of all sizes and varieties."

The landscape of old buildings, yucca, rust-colored mountains, and an eruption of pianos was just right for Squeek. She knew she had to move there but didn't know what she would do for a living. She and Roger had been fascinated by the tinseled, slurred sounds of the old uprights, and after Squeek returned to Philadelphia, Roger called back and said, "Brush up on your ragtime—we're doing a tape next week." It became the first of two cassettes that Squeek recorded on Virginia City pianos, peddling them in gift shops and by mail order. Once they braved the move, Roger took a job with the newspaper and Squeek freelanced on keyboards. On her synthesizer she provided a soundtrack for a video on the Grand Canyon and for shows at the Connecticut Science Museum Planetarium. The publicity from *Guinness* boosted her Philadelphia nightclub career, allowing her to fly back when the bank account sank. *Guinness* also yielded a surprise dividend: A convention of movie buffs at Anaheim wanted her to dance with a partner on a larger, three-octave walking piano to Ginger Rogers and Fred Astaire songs in a dress once worn by Ginger Rogers. The walking piano proved to be another springboard to adventure, and in her fifties she began a new career dancing on the convention circuit. "My partner is twenty-eight," laughed Squeek, "and I have to match him. At least from a distance. That's why I dyed my hair blond."

"I'm glad you told me. I was afraid to ask."

"It's worse than that. As a child I actually had a dream of dancing on a keyboard. Making music with my feet gives me a weird sense of power."

One of the heralded breakthroughs of the eighties was that people in upstate nowhere could grow organic vegetables and work by computer for a major conglomerate. Squeek entered the nineties by tickling the ivories nationally, by hand and by foot, while living up the street from the Bucket of Blood.

Squeek found the local musical life richer than the false fronts suggested. The Bucket of Blood actually paid its musicians, other bars encouraged tip jars, and the saloon music included dixieland, traditional jazz, banjo, ragtime piano, and country and western. At the high end was the Washo Valley String Musicale, a coterie of ladies who played chamber music and excluded Squeek. An active arts group staged operas and brought in folk music, chamber groups, and dance companies. The town turned itself over to an annual ragtime festival, with thirty pianists playing in the bars all day and a Sousa weekend every fall. The music scene in the bars switched from night to day in 1984, when Nevada enacted regressive drunken driving laws and music lovers returning to Reno and Carson City could no longer risk a whiff of beer. Musicians adapted by plunking for tourists by day and partying with locals by night.

But why would an old mining town have such a density of music in general and pianos in particular?

"Around 1875," said Squeek, "Virginia City was quite the global village. There were Chinese workers, Cornish miners, enclaves from all over Europe, and everyone needed entertainment. It ranged from community and firehouse bands to Puccini and Gilbert and Sullivan at the opera house. The Germans were so band-happy that John Philip Sousa himself came here. Gambling and prostitution were big and both liked a piano back-up. That's been the nature of this state ever since. Entertainment *is* Nevada."

But Disneyland too is a global village, and Virginia City still bothered me. With the disappearance of night business, tour buses rolled in midmorning, spewing folks who had signed up for a day's excursion. They surged through souvenir shops that called themselves "emporium" and "mercantile," had a few drafts in saloons that pretended tourists were miners from the last century, and then were trucked back to Reno or Carson City midafternoon. Ephemeral, two-dimensional, false front—I tried to convey, with a friend's license, such impressions to Squeek.

"I'd go nuts with just 700 people, pianos or not. I *like* the tourists coming in. They're not the Scottsdale set. They don't have a lot of money. A lot of them are foreign, and if I'm at a piano I like playing their music. Between the bars are lots of plastic squirrel shops, but believe it or not they help keep things the way they are. The whole town is designated a historic site on the National Register. So far there's not even a gas station or a video rental. We looked down on the tacky stuff in Jackson, then saw how quality made the place unaffordable and crowded and ugly for the rest of us. I would be a lot more upset if we had stores selling Swedish dinettes because that would mean the coming of the yuppies, people who move in instead of passing through, and the end of the Virginia City we love. Good taste has its place, but we'd rather keep this town as it is."

Kitsch as a tool of historic preservation? A new vista stretched before me in wild surmise. In Aspen I had scorned mug shops almost as much as fur stores, if for different reasons, when perhaps all along they had been secret allies. If plastic squirrels warded off more homes, I would happily wear one around my neck. We could array plastic snow globes on our sills and pitch flamingo rookeries on our lawns. If we converted jewelry stores to bazaars of refrigerator magnets, might we even get our town back? Squeek broke into these racing possibilities. "You haven't seen my piano museum yet!"

She led me outside to a converted garage with a square grand, an organ disguised as an upright, a French Pleyel of the sort Chopin might have played, and an upright she bought at an auction for fifteen dollars, having outbid the person who offered ten. "This may not look like much, but when it's finished there will be no other museum like it in the United States."

Suppressing a crack about the Newcastle Coal Museum, I asked what else she had planned.

"I'd like to build a second story and start a bed and breakfast, and then on Sunday nights have sing-alongs. This winter I plan to canvass every house and business in town and ask if they have a piano. I want to inventory the whole town."

What I lacked to be at home in Virginia City, I decided on the way back through the Great Basin in my cords and plaid, was a sense of showmanship. I had new respect for whoopee cushions and key-chain emporia, but Squeek was safe from my moving in and ruining the neighborhood. It was satisfying just to cross the apparition of crumpled ranges and oceanic valleys that, for me, *is* Nevada, to visit Squeek in a town whose vein of pianos is never played out.

Watermelon for Sale

Because I never bonded with the manicured shores of Lake Michigan where I grew up, it has been my fate to sink roots nearly everywhere else I have lingered. Installed for most of my adult years in a Colorado cabin, I nurse tendrils in Spain and Mexico, on the Atlantic seaboard, and in nearly every state in the West. When my mother remarried and moved from suburban Chicago to suburban Phoenix, I migrated annually to her place, bailing out as soon as ski season turned my formerly intimate town of Aspen into a party for glittering strangers. And a frequent pit stop on that migration was a vacation house my mother owned in northern Arizona, an attraction that surprised me because it was not, in principle, my kind of place.

From the outside the house was an undistinguished brown box fronting the seventeenth tee of a golf course. Several hundred similar houses were strewn through a ponderosa forest formerly owned by White River Apaches. A few miles

away, a twelve-mile commercial strip had skewered three traditional logging towns with chain outlets and convenience
stores. There was little to detain a desert rat.

The truth was that I had fallen in love with an interior. The
house had been built by an architect for his own use. Why he
sold it to my late stepfather I never discovered. The rooms were
perfectly proportioned, wood-paneled, anchored by a soaring
fireplace of basalt from one of the many eruptions that layered
Arizona's northern plateau. The furnishings, salvage from
my mother's and stepfather's previous lives, blended Oriental
teak and backwoods maple with unlikely finesse. My stepfather's collection of scenic oils from the thirties, illumined
with little lamps attached to the frames, overhung a spectrum
of red fabrics from a plum armchair to a watermelon sofa.
Most mysterious was an aroma compounded from pine, stone,
and dust that triggered childhood memories of summers in
Wisconsin. The house returned me to an earlier place where
I had sunk roots.

My brush with these rooms, mere overnights on my en-
trenched meander between Aspen and Phoenix, seldom included my mother's presence. She, like most owners of the
brown boxes around the golf course, came up to escape the
desert heat, months I wouldn't miss in my own home. During
one stopover I looked out a window and spotted a Western
bluebird, an omen that suggested I should get to know the
place. With the sudden, unexpected death of my mother, the
Phoenix house and the northern getaway fell to her late husband's heirs.

Coping with shock and two houses to unstuff, I looked to my
future winters. I was attached to friends in Phoenix and could
not give them up at the same time I lost my mother. Roost-
ing within the smog zone of Phoenix was also unthinkable.
And where was I to put the possessions, mine and those of my
mother that I couldn't bear to throw out and couldn't squeeze
into my cabin? On one of my daily trudges up Phoenix's

Squaw Peak—exercise so routine that sense blanked and flotsam floated to the surface—the solution struck: I should negotiate purchase of the northern getaway from my stepfather's heirs. Advantages surged. I would remain a half day's drive from friends in Phoenix. The setting, dissuasive in passing, would reveal its allure. Farther afield lay Navajo country to the north, New Mexico to the east, and the desert of my heart to the south. More immediately, I had a haven for the Phoenix possessions, including the sacred family Steinway. The plateau would be a new landscape to explore for a couple of years while I reconfigured my winters—at which point I could sell to some golfer at a profit.

I ran the idea by a usually sympathetic friend. Her eyeballs hardened. "You in the north, in the snow, on a *golf course?* You should be howling with the coyotes."

"True," I admitted. "What I'd really like is an adobe out in the cactus. But I've been all over the Arizona desert for years, and anything private where you could buy or build is threatened by development. The spot I liked best is being cased for a jetport. Anyway, I'm only keeping the place for a couple of years, until I find what's right."

"It's your life," she said.

Ironically, the threat I most feared was noise. Thinking to encourage me, a friend of my mother's who stayed through the winter boasted that a popular activity was snowmobiling on the golf course. I braced for snarling machines. When I actually moved in there were no snowmobiles to be heard. When they finally materialized one weekend, they emitted so faint a buzz that I had to run to the window to identify them. More frequent than snowmobilers were cross-country skiers who slid by like figures in a silent movie. What I didn't foresee was that in the evening, after days of calm, a tearing noise would scream right over the roof, sounding like Chicago under the el. My mother's friend, who had her pilot's license, said that the training flights emanated from a base in New Mexico, and she identified the model of each plane by its sound. Yes, she agreed, the racket was a nuisance, but they were, after all, practicing for our protection. One of the ironies of the Gulf War, for me, was that it perfected the house's silence, because the planes were all off doing what they had trained to do, over Baghdad.

The rooms' silence did approach the uncanny. As a winter resident in a summer resort, I was surrounded by empty houses. My own house sat on a corner that little traffic turned. The fairways were ordered snowfields. When I awoke in the morning and gazed from the bed, the snow was hidden below the sill and all I could see were the stout trunks and slanting branches of the ponderosas. Before I put on my glasses, the russet bark and blurred needles in the windowframe made a credible Cezanne.

I read, I wrote, I pounded the Steinway to satisfaction. Around noon I drove to the post office, the grocery, and sampled the lunch menus of every restaurant on the strip. Before driving home I got some exercise by crossing a ravine of garbage behind Safeway and climbing a hill to a firetower. I became friends with the owner of a Mexican restaurant, a woman born in Jalisco. "Nothing happens around here," she sighed. "They had a jazz concert at the high school auditorium, but nobody publicized it and nobody came. I go to the disco on Saturday nights with my girlfriend, when they have a live band. The drummer is kind of cute, but they play the same five tunes over and over. When my daughter is out of high school, I'm moving to Seattle."

Though the house was well built, it was old enough that I anticipated mechanical failures, and I wasn't surprised one morning to wake up freezing. I summoned a repairman, who informed me that the heating system was sixteen years old, so old that the only one like it he knew of was sixty miles away. He also said things like "I shunt," which he had to repeat twice before I recognized "I shouldn't." In wrestling with the problem he alternated with another repairman, who told me, "I like to build a fire of an evening," a deployment of *of* I had never heard from someone in his twenties. He also said, "Your heating system is an enigma. In the vernacular of the vulgate, it's a mess." One reason it took so long to fix, I concluded, was that the repairmen probably couldn't communicate with each other.

I took advantage of my proximity to New Mexico to visit the Malpais, a great spill of lava colonized by pines and high desert vegetation. Trails through the rock confirmed my belief that black is not an absence of color but another way of kindling the rainbow.

About once a month I visited Phoenix for a binge of companionship, or lured friends northward for a weekend. We sprawled on the red furniture, watched flames leap in the basalt fireplace, and had meals on the strip. As the snow receded one memorable Sunday in March, we hauled the Scrabble board, dictionary, and beer out to the middle of the fairway and found out what a golf course is really for.

Squirrels, ravens, and nuthatches occasionally ruffled the Cezanne, but as the snow withered and spring arrived, I realized what biologically reduced surroundings I really inhabited. Little grew beneath the ponderosas, and without an understory there was little diversity of species. Because of the area's extreme fire hazard, even the carpet of pine needles had to be raked away every year, leaving bare cinders for a yard. There were even regulations against spontaneous, combustible weeds. That premonitory bluebird was the last I saw. Because dead trees might slam on houses, snags for cavity-nesting birds were also forbidden. I was delighted when a live tree whose top had been paralyzed by lightning was colonized by a pair of Lewis' woodpeckers. I shouldn't have been surprised at the natural poverty, for this was the very plateau where Aldo Leopold, chronicling the disruptions and losses when predators were exterminated back in the twenties, worked out some of the basics of ecology.

I spent two winters and two springs in the house by the seventeenth tee. I intersected very little with golfers, for I was gone before all but the hardiest revved up their carts. I had forgotten that I only intended to occupy the house for two years when, exactly two years later, I summoned a woman who called herself a real-a-tor and put the house on the market. We signed a contract, then she pulled a yellow sign out of her trunk and hammered it under the pines. The multiple listing crew showed up next week in a dozen cars and I waited outside, as instructed, for the three minutes it took them to appraise the offering. I reentered it to find business cards strewn like bird droppings on the kitchen counter, and the house stank of perfume for the next two hours.

The house may not be so easy to sell, even to a golfer, for yellow signs are sanctioned weeds throughout the neighborhood. Was it the economic downturn, or was even the summer crowd bored? Not since my suburban childhood had I lived whole seasons as a kind of air plant, detachable from where I was. I had failed to pry out the plateau's endearing secrets and merely gained, feeling guilty, a few platitudes from my own interior. Inside and outside have to converse, and the spirit nods when living quarters are more interesting than what lies beyond them. Obsessions—reading, writing, playing the piano, work, or indulgence—are more vital when occasionally interfered with. A fire-protected ponderosa forest is sensory deprivation, even when compared to a subdivided desert. Without social props, desert rats seeking life zones should aim low. As for the house's interior, I am as attached to it as ever, but except for the sacred Steinway, it too is for sale, watermelon sofa and all.

Blue

Its unreality first struck me when I was five, visiting my aunt and uncle in their dilapidated shingle house outside Omaha. I had been warned not to venture beyond the lawn into the great woods, an oaken tangle thick with foxes and poison ivy that fell to the Missouri River. But even inside the house everything was alarming and strange, and among the knick-knacks and souvenirs on my aunt's shelf, silhouetted against a diamond-paned window that gave onto huge trees, was a blue bottle that crystallized the wooded darkness and all that lay beyond. Out in the open, the color surrounded me unnoticed; now it confronted me for the first time, reduced to an essence. Its coolness frightened me, like some revelation that would forever recede as it lured one forward.

The depth of a blue depends less on its shade than a lumi-nescence suggestive of distance, isolation, something inex-pressibly lost. I have seen it since in the sky behind the haloed saints in twelfth-century stained glass. It floods through the windows if you are driving through moonlit snow and douse the lights. It glows between black calligraphy in the canvases of Roualt. From a turn in a lime-bleached Aegean street a blue building will swim up like a sea cave. It is the glacier's heart. Our American lyrical sadness is the blues.

It was a shock of recognition to come upon the first photographs from space, showing our planet sailing the black void in swirls of luminous, marbleized blue. Blue, it turns out, has the highest energy in the visible spectrum, and is the color most intensely scattered by Earth's atmosphere. Oxygen was not an original component of our air. It built up slowly with the emergence of green plants three billion years ago. Through the process of photosynthesis, plants take carbon dioxide from the air and give back oxygen. Along with its dominance by nitrogen, our blue-scattering atmosphere is a balance between oxygen from living plants and carbon dioxide from organic matter's decay. Green may be the color of life on the surface, but the color of life from space, at least for this planet, is blue.

It wasn't until I reached the Pacific coast of Baja California that I realized how that blue, even as it embraces our home, remains unearthly, luring one forward, unattainable. I held it in my hand, in the form of a lobster shell fresh from the sea. It was little more than a claw and a few square inches of body thrown up by the tide, murderously brittle, but radiating a light from turquoise to cobalt. Hundreds of miles of igneous jeep-rattling tracks led back up the peninsula, with hundreds more miles of pavement to my windowsill, but I had to try. I nestled the fragments in wadded toilet paper, stuffed them into an economy-sized coffee jar, then cradled the jar in my parka so it could ride all the way home in suspension. Weeks later I set the jar on my table, cautiously unscrewed the lid and pulled out the paper, expecting little more than a blue ash. Each piece had miraculously survived, oxidized by the very air that sustains us to a pale and sarcastic pink.

Desert Diorama

The guest bedroom bookshelves of my mother's house near Phoenix contain one space that dwarfs the others. In the normal shelves of this room I have occupied season after season, year after year, I have lodged my growing collection of books about the desert. In the gap between them, doubtless intended for art books or significant urns, I have arranged the coils, spikes, rondures, serrations, and globes of iron, bark, carapace, industrial porcelain, shell, needles, and cheap china I have hauled back from the desert itself. At first I stashed the debris there merely to sheild it from the withering gaze of my mother. Gradually it occurred to me that my souvenirs comment on the desert more sharply than the books that surround them and that my midden is reproducing the snarls of a desert rat's subconscious.

Dominating by sheer complication is a coil of chain that joins a barbed anchor to what looks like a small bridge trestle. The trestle, in fact, discovered me, for I was hiking an arroyo

below the McDowell Mountains and my boot struck something stranger and more instantly chilling than anything I had
previously encountered. Perhaps it was only that I stubbed
iron when I expected stone. The trestle alone showed above
the sand and it was a moment before I identified this as my
first leghold trap. Poking it with a stick to make sure the clamp
was shut, I yanked out the rest—five feet of chain, then, with
more tugging, the anchor. The clamp was four inches across,
ample for a hiker's instep or a coyote's paw. I shook off the
sand and crammed it awkwardly into my daypack, glad to
have rid the desert of one more contrivance. The trap now reminds me less of that quick chill than of the arroyo itself, a
drainage that has gone from ambushing fur to repairing the
species that traps, for it is now the site of the westernmost
Mayo Clinic.

Nearly as large as the trap, competing with it for dominance
on the shelf, is the shell of a desert tortoise I found even closer
to home, on Mummy Mountain. I have seen very few desert
tortoises over years of hiking, though many may have posed
as rocks as I passed. It seems suspicious that one of the few
live tortoises I have run across was on the same section of
the same mountain, the previous year. The same individual?
Surely a close relation. The backbone is incised with thirteen
rough rhombuses and a fringe of twenty-three smaller ones—
unlikely numbers for an effect so symmetrical. Almost half the
covering plates are left, in pieces that fit the sectioned bone,
and a lose plate can be held to the light. The translucence
is pleasant enough, a kind of smudged amber, but it is difficult to imagine it being forged into combs and snuff boxes.
Decorative tortoise shell comes from such sea creatures as
the hawksbill turtle—or, more recently, from plastic—and the
desert tortoise is being threatened for less aesthetic reasons,
such as the development through which I trespassed.

Surely the shelf's most eccentric items are two pre-Columbian ceramic animal heads I retrieved from a wastebasket in

Santa Fe. I had been sent by a magazine to watch the firing
of a ceramic plate at the Santa Clara Pueblo. It was between
Christmas and New Year's, the lodges were filled, and I was
stashed in a gallery that traded in Native American arts. When
I asked about the heads in the wastebasket, I was told that
they were roughly 1,500 years old, had passed through Indian,
Mexican, and Anglo hands, and had been smuggled into the
United States on a private yacht only to be dropped on a gallery floor. Not to worry, said my informant; such pieces were
common enough, not especially valuable.

It was hard to know what animals these glazes were supposed to represent, for they were featureless and shaped like
elongated gourds. Each had a thin, squared-off ridge line that
ran from the back of the skull over the face and around the
snout. But it was not common to me that such objects, however standard in their day, had survived fifteen centuries of
neglect and nefarious trading only to end up in a gallery john,
and I crammed them into my battered daypack. They were
two of the three broken ceramics I took home, the third being
a fragment of red glaze showing a bear claw, the most interesting remnant of the plate whose firing I had driven hundreds of miles to see, only to watch it blow up in a gust of
wind.

A less fragile ceramic, nestled against a bookshelf wall,
is a small white porcelain cylinder with a hole through the
middle and a deep groove on the outside. It is a phone line
insulator from southeast Utah. In 1910 the U.S. Forest Service
strung the first phone line to the isolated ranching community
of Boulder from the remote town of Escalante, swerving and
sheering through ridge and canyon. Insulators were attached
to live trees, to juniper posts, to metal poles in open ground,
then connected with galvanized wire. Boulder is believed to
be the last town in the contiguous forty-eight states to receive
mail by mule, over a trail that followed the phone line. The
mule trains were discontinued in 1926, but the phone line

remained in service until 1955, when Bell Telephone ran its towers and wires elsewhere. A portion of the old mail and phone route guided our hiking party over a plateau between drainages, and a loose insulator at my feet became ballast in my pack.

Rounding out the collection's human artifacts is a slightly charred salad plate, scalloped, with a mustard-colored ornamental circle around the center, part of a hotel service and practically unbreakable. I had read in the *Arizona Republic*, to my horror, that the Hermosa Inn had been gutted by fire. One of the few resorts that retained the intimate, low-keyed, aromatic ranch atmosphere of Phoenix in the thirties and forties, Hermosa Inn had begun as the private home of an artist named Lon Megargee. Few remember the name but almost everyone has seen a series of paintings he did for a long-gone Arizona brewery called A-1. The most famous, "Black Bart," shows a barber shop whose wall features a poster advertising A-1 Beer and another proclaiming, BLACK BART, $5,000 REWARD DEAD OR ALIVE, with a picture of Black Bart. Leaning back in the barber chair, hand on a cocked six-shooter, is Black Bart himself, awaiting the removal of his identifying beard, while standing in back of the chair, shaving mug in one hand and straight edge in the other, is a hard-thinking barber. Will the barber go for the throat and the reward, or will Black Bart shoot him first? Such alternatives float through the observer, nursing an A-1, though my Phoenix barber, who has a copy of "Black Bart" on his wall, spends more time wondering whether this is the only barber in the world who can lather and shave at the same time, or whether Megargee knew nothing about barbering. Another painting in the series, "Cowboy's Dream," shows a wrangler asleep on a woman-shaped cloud, his hand on a branding iron whose 1-A, seared into cow flesh, will reverse itself into the brand of the beer.

These paintings, and others more serious if less lucrative, brought in enough money that in 1938 Megargee hand-built a sprawling house full of secret passages. On his death it was turned into a small inn. Tucked away on a quiet residential street that retained desert vegetation even as greater Phoenix obliterated it for miles beyond, the Hermosa catered to guests almost as reclusive as Megargee. But the management must have realized that its wood and adobe lounge had the liveliest acoustics in town, for a few years before the blaze they hired the valley's best jazz pianist. Other musicians showed up to jam, night-clubbers began making obscure turns down Palo Cristi Road, and the fire's most immediate effect was to deliver a body blow to Phoenix jazz.

I went to inspect the damage a few days after the fire and found the walls still standing, surrounded by a new chain-link fence. The gate was open, no one was about, and I ventured in. The stench was dry, bitter, unbearable. Every room was gutted. I toured rooms I had never seen before—the kitchen, the pantry, the office—then stared up into the little tower where Megargee painted, drawing a rope ladder up after him to get away from admirers who pursued him to his very lair. There was nothing but charred rooms to see—except for boxes of china, oddly the only objects not thrown away. Most were blackened beyond salvation, but I selected the least damaged salad plate as a souvenir of Megargee, of the dying guest ranch culture, of jazz that is dying more slowly, of a walk through a burnt building.

Among these memento mori by my bed are several specimens of my favorite desert object, the cactus boot. These are not just holes in cactus, they are holes in logic, gaps that survive what held them. Just after nesting season, woodpeckers and flickers gouge the pulp of saguaros, scooping out their next home in a few minutes. To protect itself from infection, the cactus caulks the hole with scar tissue. The little cave is sealed tight by the time the excavators are ready to start a new family. The original birds inhabit the holes for only a season or two, then carve new holes, freeing the old ones for a range of species from elf and screech owls to martins and fly-catchers. When the holes become too cluttered for birds at all, rats and mice take over. After a century or two the saguaro will keel over, losing first its pulp, then, after a few decades, its ribs. Finally only bits of scar tissue, crusts of old theft, lie kicking on the desert floor. Tons of living flesh are outlived by the hulls of absence. Shaped like pears, kidneys, scows, old shoes, these are the boots in which nothing walks.

Surrounding this composition of objects that summon memories is a blur of refuse whose origins are forgotten. Clusters of needles from dead cacti pose like black spiders. There is a gray gourd, perfectly round and large as a softball. Are sand dollars really desert currency? At least they are from Baja California, where the desert meets the sea. The sole note of glitter in all this dun is a Cub Scout belt buckle, fake gold with a blue fleur-de-lis and the name Tony scratched on the back. I suppose Tony became uncinched on the trail, though it is more satisfying to imagine him being devoured by a bear who spit out the buckle.

This large and filthy shelf nearly stops the vision, but for the imagination it opens a window through all these books, back into the desert. This version of the desert is pure evocation, disjointed, with unsteady contours. The souvenirs of man do look rawer, sadder, more dated. They summon individual defeats or ways of life that have passed, while even nature's bones seem vows of renewal. The same objects confirm that man the transient, with his bookshelves and hospitals and conflagrations, is overcoming the creatures that conquered drought. Weak and contradictory, such deductions fade in the sheer wealth of detail that a few objects can bring forth—a prospect that overwhelms when one considers the desert's own collection. In the swirl of this detritus the mind blanks, leaving a diorama of sun-baked madeleines receding under dust that filters in from the desert outside. The desert will not succeed in burying them soon, but that does not stop it from trying.

A Cactus of Our Times

The odds have always been against being a saguaro cactus. Only one out of every 275,000 seeds grows to maturity. Sensitive tots, they must begin life in the shade of a nurse tree. They take 25 years to grow the first two feet. They don't branch until they are 75 years old, and only reach true adulthood at 100 years. At full growth, a saguaro can top fifty feet, weigh more than ten tons, and live 250 years. Until recently, life under such conditions has precluded travel.

A few years ago I was able to follow, first from newspaper reports, then in person, the odyssey of one contemporary saguaro from origin to conclusion. A road through an exclusive Phoenix suburb was being four-laned to accommodate commuters, and the neighborhood was not amused. In a stroke of conciliation, the highway department proposed a median strip of native plants that would transform the four-lane into a desert parkway, pleasing to resident and winter visitor alike. A diversion canal outside Yuma, meanwhile, was being cut through virgin desert, and the larger cacti could be salvaged and relocated in the median. The solution seemed to placate all parties.

I followed in the paper how the lateral roots of the saguaros were severed, leaving little but the taproots. The cacti then rode on their sides more than 200 miles to Phoenix. A few were inadvertently smashed by a road crew unused to vegetable matter of several tons, but enough survived that I watched them being hoisted onto the median by large yellow machines that held up traffic. Without root systems to keep them vertical, most of the saguaros were propped by boards on four sides.

Even when the planks were removed, the neat alternation of saguaros, cholla, agaves, and prickly pear showed the heavy hand of the planner. It may be fringe sensibility to attribute feeling to plants, but I couldn't help wondering whether the saguaros didn't feel in their fibers the difference between the peace outside Yuma, where their roots sprawled at will, and this cramped strip where gaseous machines rushed on either side at all hours. Almost every Monday I saw mangled prickly pears and agaves, presumably where people returning home after weekend closing hours had veered onto the median.

One Saturday evening, returning from a country club where I had played dinner piano for a Planned Parenthood banquet, the car ahead leapt across my lane, narrowly missing me, bowled down the median flattening two chollas and a yucca, passed straight through a saguaro, cleared the two opposing lanes, and came to a rocking halt on a side street. I pulled up behind it. The couple had just left the same fundraiser, where the man had overindulged and turned over the wheel to his date. She was unfamiliar with the car, had tried to shift into overdrive, and hit reverse. The couple was unhurt and the car suffered nothing more than a crumpled hood, stripped gears, and a smashed windshield. But the saguaro lay in pieces.

Because the saguaro was just beginning to branch, I figured that it had been born close to the year when Arizona became a state, in 1912. Its midsection, dark as the asphalt and invisible on approach, blocked one lane of traffic and was the next potential accident. I intended to stand in front of it, motioning traffic away until a police car came by. The next car, it happened, was a taxi. When I pointed to the cactus, it slowed, nudged the pulp to the curb as if such bulldozing were standard, and sped off. The next morning I went back to see what remained. Only skid marks showed where the sedan had gone out of control, and the saguaro had been removed to wherever our tax dollars dispose of our mistakes.

Phoenician Shipwrecks

As Mars was once thought to be, Phoenix is crisscrossed by canals. Except for what remains of its desert setting, canals may be Phoenix's most distinguishing feature. Varying little, pooling a personality, they make soft incisions through what surrounds them. As you jockey through traffic dizzied by small businesses and their signs, numbed by miles of ranch homes and convenience stores, your eyes will flicker coolly down what seems an open tunnel of water. Receding parallels of packed desert sand, twenty feet wide, clean of vegetation, frame an even, sky-reflecting flow. Glimpses of joggers and cyclists along the banks indicate that there is still human life without combustion. For all their sterility, the canals command moving water and thus retain more mystery than anything else in the valley. Because they so prominently display what makes a desert city possible, it would seem that to get to the bottom of the canals would be to get to the bottom of Phoenix.

Part of the canals' mystique is that some of their routes predate Phoenix by nearly two millennia. Beginning around 200 A.D., Hohokam Indians, using hand-held digging tools, moved tons of earth and engineered the largest pre-Columbian irrigation system in the Western Hemisphere. Some 250 miles of canals fanned like tufts of hair from the Salt River, irrigating several thousand acres of corn, squash, beans, pumpkins, and cotton. Having reached a population of 20,000, the Hohokam abandoned the Salt River Valley around A.D. 1400, possibly because they had depleted the soil.

For the next four centuries the drainage cooked in the sun, its canal system choked with the debris of flash floods. The dormancy lasted until just after the Civil War, when gold miners burst into the Arizona Territory. Migrants to the West Coast passed through the valley. U.S. Army forts were established to the northwest at Prescott and Wickenberg, and upstream from Phoenix at Fort McDowell, to fend off Apaches. Miners, migrants, and soldiers all needed to be fed. In 1867 a scheming ex-Confederate soldier named Jack Swilling responded with the Swilling Irrigation and Canal Company. Using Mexican labor he retrenched many of the old Hohokam canals. Alfalfa for horses and grain for persons soon flowed from the Salt River Valley to the forts. So responsive was the soil that miners and migrants, safe from attack, grabbed shovels and went what was soon called "canal crazy."

The founding of the Swilling Irrigation Company was, in essence, the founding of Phoenix. An American grid of streets was imposed on the snaking, geologically determined weft of canals. Canals bred canals, and Anglo machines were able to tap the Salt River farther upstream than had been possible for the Hohokam. The river's wild floods clearly couldn't be allowed to roar through the reworked water system, returning it to waste, and a canal users' association called the Salt River Project was organized to brake the flow. Private and territorial boosters lobbied for passage of the National Reclamation Act of 1902 and landed a federal grant for what is still the world's tallest masonry dam, eighty miles upstream on the Salt River. Named for a president eager to replumb the West, Roosevelt Dam was completed in 1911, one year before Arizona became a state. It was eventually joined by three more dams on the Salt River and two on the Rio Verde, which meets the Salt just above Phoenix.

The history of Phoenix, from outpost through oasis to ele-phantiasis, is written in channeled water. With the completion of Granite Reef Dam in 1908, just upstream from Phoenix, it was possible to split the entire flow of the Salt River to either side of the river itself, so that 100 percent was siphoned into man-made canals and zero percent maintained the riverbed. Changing attitudes toward the canals present an oblique but curious record of how America expressed itself on its driest fringe and remind us that, even in the desert, water remains a primary figure for the human unconscious.

The Salt River Project consolidated a system from canals that farmers and water companies had dug on their own. This sys-tem incorporates 131 miles of main canals that deliver water to 880 miles of subsidiary canals, called laterals. From there, it is the prerogative of every recipient, or group of recipients, to take the water through any system they have rigged and to irrigate what they will. As alfalfa, the main original crop, was replaced by citrus groves and then by residential neighbor-hoods, the delivery points remained exactly where they were. The urbanization of an agricultural area with its irrigation system intact created a genuine novelty: a desert city of canals.

As Phoenix started to expand into its farms and orchards, life became intimate with the flow of water. The riparian zone of the Salt River, to be sure, died at a blow when Granite Reef Dam cut off the flow, but in another sense, the river habitat splintered and fissioned through the canals. The laterals were open ditches with culverts where streets passed over. Shady

Fremont cottonwoods, the dominant tree along the Salt River, fanned through the new water system, along with willows and tamarisk. From the twenties through the fifties, when dude ranches were romantic getaways for easterners who rode horses into the desert, the outdoor life of locals centered on the canals. No one yet had private swimming pools, and in summer, when water still ran cool from the reservoirs, children learned to swim in the canals. Swings hung from cottonwood branches over the water. Arizona's native fish used the system freely, and people fished from bridges and canal banks for bass, crappie, and catfish. Eric Bergersen, who later became a fish biologist, remembers a bloom of silverfin shad from Saguaro Lake that poured into the laterals and got stranded during irrigation on the lawns. "They stank for awhile, then they became good fertilizer." And where there were roads instead of trees along the bank, people skimmed along the canals on aquaplanes and water skis, holding a rope from a car.

Living with the canals meant accepting the risk of open water. More perilous than the canals were the laterals, where children splashed through the undergrowth and dared each other to swim through culverts that often had no air at all and could be clogged with brush in the middle. Child drownings were a summer staple. When water spilled over a canal bank, flooding a neighborhood so that water covered the baseboard plugs and people worried about electrocution, a friend of mine became a teenage hero by digging a trench in a bank farther down, which the water itself widened on its way back into the system. "Instead of being grateful," he says, "the Salt River Project was mad as hell that I had violated their sacred canal bank." Water skiing at fifty miles per hour in a canal fifty feet wide took skill, and those who veered into the banks came to grief. Neighborhoods considered the canals their social centers, and people accepted the dangers in the same way they tolerated swimming with dead cats, dogs, and snakes. Adults staked ropes over the banks to provide sure places to get out, watched over their children, and taught them safe swimming. Most of the resorts were beyond the canal system, but Frank Lloyd Wright designed a textile block bridge over the Arizona Canal to harmonize architecturally with his Arizona Biltmore, and the canal-side Ingleside Resort had canoes, a romantic promenade, and a waterfall.

Through the end of the fifties, Phoenix grew in leafy, low-keyed neighborhoods. Even when houses took over citrus groves, many of the orange and grapefruit trees were left standing. With the sixties came walled subdivisions full of houses with backyard pools, and the mentality shifted abruptly. Canals were now that murky area over the wall, slightly mysterious and decidedly unsafe. There was a push from mothers, taken up by the newspapers, to cover the laterals because children could drown there, and the laterals disappeared into buried pipes. Canals were literally screened out of peoples' lives, and the Salt River Project, flowing with opinion, put out messages on the radio and in the schools not to swim in them. As the canals became demonized, people who lived in the immaculate subdivisions threw their trash over the wall into what had been communal playgrounds, and once the canals had become corridors of garbage, there was a clamor from the very perpetrators to clean them up.

The Salt River Project had never been happy to see water mandated for agricultural, municipal, and industrial uses being transpired into the sky by cottonwood trees. The political climate was ripe for defoliation. Cottonwoods, tamarisk, and willows along the banks were felled and plants were cleared. Annuals such as weeds and wildflowers were poisoned. Service roads were elevated on either side of the banks, and the porous interiors of the canals were lined with gunite, a brew of sand, cement, and water sprayed three inches thick onto a wire mesh. People who fished during the purification remember that when there were cottonwoods on one side and gunite banks on the other, all the fish were under the cotton-woods. In 1973, the Salt River Project inserted steps painted yellow every fifty yards along the canal banks, but only as emergency exits for people who fell in. By the time the de-vegetation and lining of the canals were complete, the man-made but luxuriant meanders that had softened and socialized Phoenix reflected only gunite, phone poles, utility wires, and sky.

Even as the canals were sanitized and agricultural lands were diced for tract housing, water continued to arrive at the de-livery points, creating a system unique to any American city. A citizen whose home sits in a former alfalfa field or citrus grove may sign up for water to flood his yard. Water arrives every fourteen days from April through September and every twenty-eight days the rest of the year. Deliveries are measured in time, and a typical fifth-of-an-acre lot will take forty-five minutes of water, or 27,000 gallons. Water is rotated through the network of laterals on a twenty-four-hour basis, and each lateral services several blocks of a city. Recipients are respon-sible for opening the valves in their yards when their turn comes, whether it is during the day or in the middle of the night. They must also maintain any ditches, gates, valves, or berms on their properties.

By this subterranean means, the ghost of the Salt River still holds a neighborhood together or pulls it apart. Blocks scheduled for night deliveries will sometimes keep vigil at someone's house over coffee or drinks to supervise a smooth passage from yard to yard. Those unable or unwilling to twist their valves at odd hours may hire zanjeros whose function is to turn valves on cue and watch that water doesn't spill over. Spillage is a serious offense, for water does not merely moisten the ground; it steeps in the yard, swamps the grass, turns flower beds to gruel. Homeowners who let their allot-ment escape have been responsible for up to 40,000 gallons of rogue water that can destroy a neighbor's den, chew up the streets, and divert cars into each other. Letting water run wild is a misdemeanor, and as a Salt River Project brochure observes, "Once water is ordered, it can not be sent back." The Salt River Project's official obligation ends at the delivery point, and they try to make neighborhoods themselves deal with local problems, such as a neighbor who doesn't clean his ditch. They have, however, been forced to hire field representatives who try to get neighbors to cooperate and who have authority to close the headgate if a neighborhood just lets the water run. One neighborhood was about to be cut off when the flooding was traced to a tied monkey with no diversion but the valve.

Even after sterilization, the system itself remained strange enough to spark incident. A bar friend of mine was deluged with Esther Williams memorabilia when it was reported that he had driven home after last call, rolled out of his car, and landed face down during irrigation night. He might have drowned on his front lawn if his roommate hadn't heard the splash.

In another neighborhood a canal-loving friend, who nearly died as a child when a lateral pulled him under a sluice gate, was throwing rocks into a gunite-lined canal with buddies at the age of fifteen. He spotted what looked like "a shoulder and a cowlick" drifting slowly in the middle of the water. Unsure of the object, he chucked a rock, hit the cowlick, and heard a thud so dull he was sure he had hit a man or mannikin. He ran home and interrupted a card game between his mother and his uncle with the story. The uncle, half convinced, called the police. By the time they caught up with the object, it had gone through a lock at Central Avenue and resurfaced as a fully clothed adult male. The body was still mid-canal, and police and firemen tried to reach him from the bank with hooks. Tom's uncle, disgusted with squeamishness in uniform, plunged in and dragged the body to shore. Dressed in a suit, tie, and wingtip shoes, the victim sported an expensive watch and an unrecognizable face. Because the year was 1971, the zenith of the mob-related Arizona land-fraud murders, Tom was sure that the man had been done in and dumped. The police report stated that the deceased, overdressed as he may have been, was repairing his car on a service road when he fell backward into the canal, and his death was declared an accident.

Such larks are the exception, and most of today's adventure is suffered by those who unwittingly drive through neighborhoods toward a canal to find that streets come irrationally to a dead end, hook into residential circles, or double back on themselves as grid turns to labyrinth. Peering into those labyrinths from the canal banks, one sees that the backyards are furnished with endless permutations of swing sets, patio furniture, oleander hedges, barbecues, and small pools. The neatness and lack of eccentricity suggest that Phoenicians have become a passive lot, content to tend their gardens, unconcerned that their river has been diverted into most undiverting canals.

There are, however, active Phoenicians who have looked urban dissolution in the face and seen the canals as potential deliverance. They have a built-in constituency in the many citizens who walk, jog, or bike along the canal banks, both for exercise and for nonmotorized transportation, braving vistas of cinderblocks, employee parking, dumpsters, and windowless office backs. In the fourteen contiguous communities serviced by the Salt River Project canals, a battalion of civic groups has proposed a transformation of the canals to include landscaping, drinking fountains, pocket parks, equestrian trails, waterside rests, pedestrian bridges, islands, underpasses, illumination, signs to tell you what street you're crossing, pedestrian-activated traffic lights, integration with canal-side housing projects, public art, decorative paving, a mini-railroad, restoration of an old waterfall, and call boxes for emergencies. Renovated canals are seen as a way of linking greater Phoenix while each community projects its own identity. Scottsdale would specialize in outdoor cafes and shops fronting the canal. Gilbert would feature a farmers' market. It seems apt that Sharon Southerland, president of the Metropolitan Canal Alliance that coordinates the planning groups, bonded with the unreformed canals as a child, nearly drowning when she tried to swim through a pipe.

Southerland sees the canal projects as a link to the city's origins. Archaeological studies, she says, keep raising the percentage of the main canal routes that follow those dug by the Hohokam, a figure now approaching 70 percent. Modern Phoenix is made possible by the canals: they are drinking water, irrigation, life. With grant money from various communities and the National Endowment for the Arts, the College of Archaeology and Design at Arizona State University has come up with guidelines that have been endorsed, sometimes in extravagant language, by public officials. Said the mayor of Scottsdale, "I think the canal banks can be almost as great an attraction as the ocean in San Diego, even in August." Said the assistant professor of architecture who is spearheading the plan, "We want to create a memorable image so that people think of us like other memorable cities throughout the world, such as Paris and Vienna." Most observers agree that it will take more than well-trimmed water to turn Phoenix into Paris or Vienna, and a more reasonable—and interesting— perspective is offered by Cindy Ashton, also of the Metropolitan Canal Alliance. "Someday people are going to fly into Phoenix and there will be green lines winding through town. It's an *aerial* identity that people will want to explore on the ground." Southerland is quick to add, "But we're looking at it not as a tourist attraction, but as a way to improve our own lives."

Beyond agreeing on the details and then paying for them, a

major impediment is the Salt River Project's system of service roads. Says Southerland, "You can't do anything on the banks that gets in the way of trucks going by. The canals are also corridors for electric lines. Near the water, for instance, we can have planters but not rooted trees. We're looking at hydroseeding and native grass right up to the edge. That's what it looks like in the spring now, until the Salt River Project poisons the vegetation." While Southerland claims a good working relationship with the Salt River Project, she also bluntly stated what I had suspected. "The Salt River Project uses us as a buffer with the public. It's good PR."

To see how citizen greening of the canals sat with the Salt River Project, I left the Metropolitan Canal Alliance, which was camped in the temporary headquarters of the Phoenix Junior League, upstairs in a shopping mall, and negotiated traffic to a sprawling office building set in acres of parking. The Salt River Project does not just run one valley's canal system. It is part owner of various coal-fired power plants, including the Navajo Generating Plant that had just been ordered to stop smogging the Grand Canyon; it generates hydroelectric power on the Salt, Verde, and Colorado rivers; it partially owns the controversial Palo Verde Nuclear Generating Station; and it is the third largest power utility in the United States. Meeting me by appointment were Paul Cherrington and John Egan, respectively manager of water transmission and superintendent of media relations.

Cherrington and Egan led me through a warren of polished halls to a sanctum I had hoped to see, the control room of the canal system. Theaterlike, its banks of manned computers faced a curved wall of screens that showed the canal networks north and south of the Salt River, along with a screen called a water log, which scrolls through the canals' measuring devices and can report the precise amount of water at any given point. Cherrington explained that the Salt River Project's zanjeros in the field take orders from farmers, residents, and

water treatment plants, then a water master determines each
day how much water needs to be drawn from the storage dams
and in what ratio it should be divided at Granite Reef Dam
into the system's two parts. "The control system is getting very
automated. Every gate out there is telemetered back to the
computer terminals here." He bent to an unoccupied terminal
and began pressing keys. "We can open a gate just by putting
the cursor here and pushing this button on the left."

"During summer thunderstorms, this is a very interesting
place to be," said John Egan. "We have people getting information from the U.S. Weather Service radar, which happens
to be just down the hall. There are water masters taking flood
water in and water masters keeping the canals from overflow-
ing. It's a real madhouse." A quite unmad calm marked our
visit, but it was a calm in which one could dispatch a smart
bomb.

Once we had retreated to a generic office, I asked Cherrington and Egan their opinion of canal reformation. "I'm
chairman of the Salt River Project's Canal Multiple Use Co-
ordinating Center, which entertains all the various proposals,"
said Cherrington. "You have to realize, of course, that our job
is to deliver water, which belongs to the users, not the Salt
River Project, and part of our job is keeping the canals clean."
Growth of vegetation in the canals, he explained, had been a
problem since their inception, because the combination of silt
and sunlight grows algae, moss, and weeds that can use up
to half the water and choke the channels themselves. Canals
were historically cleaned by stopping the water and clear-
ing the bottom with horse-drawn scrapers. The first canals
to have roads on both sides were dredged, full, with ship
chains hauled by trucks. Eventually chemicals were introduced, which are more effective on plant life but tended to
worry people who received their drinking water from one of
the canals' seven water treatment plants. The thirty-day dry-
up was instituted by Phoenix. In this operation the canals, in

rotation, are emptied and the Salt River Project gets in, sprays gunite, and scours them.

Two recent additions to the cleaning process may aid the forces of transformation. One is the telescoop, a long-armed robot that can clean the canal from one side, freeing the other side to be vegetated. But even more uptown is the white amur, a vegetarian carp from Asia, commercially grown in Arkansas. Weighing seven pounds when released, an amur can eat its weight in vegetable matter daily and in fifteen years may grow up to five feet long and weigh seventy-five pounds. Arizona's ravaged native fish are protected in that only sterile amurs are released, and amur-proof grates keep them within the system. Fifteen thousand amurs were dumped into the canals between 1889 and 1992, and they have proved the cheapest and safest canal cleaner yet—though dry-ups, machines, and chemicals downstream from the treatment plants are all still used in changing combinations.

Now that I was up to speed on canal cleaning, Cherrington addressed my question. "We have a fifty-foot right-of-way from the highline of the canal, but we need only fifteen or twenty feet for equipment. We have agreed, in certain cases, to give up one side of the canal, and will give up both sides if the city in question will pick up the tab for maintaining that part of the canal. We resist trees within fifteen feet of the canal, and we resist boats. But the trend now is toward attractive canals, and there's pressure to build things like the San Antonio Riverwalk."

I found it curious that both the Metropolitan Canal Alliance and the Salt River Project had referred to the precedent set by the popular Riverwalk in San Antonio, Texas—and both agreed that Riverwalk, though admirable, was puny and artificial in comparison. Riverwalk was only a few blocks long and water was diverted to it strictly for effect. The Phoenix canals, by comparison, were 181 miles long if you included an extra 50 miles of canals that remained outside the Salt River

Project system. That was 362 miles of canal bank: no other American city had anything like it.

I left the Salt River Project tallying the phases the Phoenix canal system had gone through: Hohokam canals; canals dredged in the last century following the Hohokam routes; canal consolidation under the Salt River Project; canals as social centers teeming with natural growth; sterilization and ban on public recreation following the advent of walled sub-divisions; now plans to convert the canals to highly structured, multiple-use greenbelts. The revival of recreation at the canals was hardly a return to the era of swings hung over swimming holes from cottonwood limbs, although many people planning the reconstituted canals lived their childhoods during that period and might unconsciously be trying to reproduce it. The new focus on the canals was rehabilitation by master plan, with every planter positioned, every cafe table in conformity with rules of access, every bypath checked for liability, every inspiration—however lovely—thrashed out by committee. It was hard to be spontaneous in the age of litigation. The improvements, if brought to fruition, would vastly enliven the waterways that cross the Salt River Valley so bald and alike. And in continuing to reflect America in controlled water, the plans project, unavoidably, the age of shopping malls, of political compromise, of safety, of bond elections, and of social correctness and urban design.

Of course all the assorted forms of canal craziness overlook what Phoenix and the Salt River Valley might have been if the water—even part of the water—had been left in the river. It was, to be sure, the Hohokam, and not the Anglo, who dipped the first straw, but the Hohokam lacked the storage dams to gain total control. If enough water had been left to maintain riverbanks of cottonwood and willow, with habitat for tanagers, otters, and herons, the Salt River might have made a luxuriant focus for a romantic city of canals. But total control, once gained, was exercised, reducing the riverbed to a waste

of gravel operations and blowing trash. A proposal to restore a
section of the river, again with highly structured landscaping,
was voted down, primarily because it seemed to tax all of
greater Phoenix to benefit one area. During the spectacular
flood years of 1978 and 1980, when record rains and snowmelt
funneled water even five storage dams couldn't handle, water
poured through the bed of the Salt River like lava, severing
all but two bridges, undermining the interstate, infuriating
commuters, and bringing smiles to the faces of river lovers.
While the water was unable to rouse a long-dead ecosystem,
it was viscerally thrilling to watch that raw, sinewed power
even while stalled bumper to bumper on a gridlocked bridge.
It hinted the Phoenix that might have been.

Phoenicians have accepted for generations the theft of their
river, usually without a thought, and the few who take offense
vent their spleen on the agency with the power, the Salt River
Project. One such person—the one who incurred the wrath of
the Salt River Project by breaching one of their canal banks
as a teenager, and who returns the sentiment—is Tim Means,
who later gave up managership of a Phoenix Jack-in-the-Box
to become a guide on the Colorado River. I once had the
pleasure of touring the Phoenix Zoo with Tim. At one point
the displays parted to reveal, across Mill Avenue, the corpo-
rate headquarters of the Salt River Project. As if reading a
sign in front of a cage, Tim extemporized, "Salt River Project.
Projectio Fluminis Salarius. Endemic to Arizona, where it is
the most dangerous predator. Exhibits beaverlike compulsion
to impound moving water. Favored prey species include wild
rivers and tax dollars. DO NOT FEED."

My own canal madness was the idée fixe that to get to the
bottom of the canals was to get to the bottom of Phoenix—
an act best accomplished during dry-up. Because the canals
are public, and it is a global vice to dispose of unwanted
objects in moving water, for eleven months each year the

canal is fed a rich diet that is exposed when the sections are dried for repairs. As with ski resorts, where locals walk under the chairlifts when the snow melts to see what has fallen out of suspended pockets, Phoenix scavengers prowl the canals for booty when the sluice gates shut. Reported finds have included vending machines, refrigerators, tires, chassis, couches, money, jewelry, guns, needles and, for the first to arrive, edible fish. In answer to my question, John Egan, PR director for the Salt River Project, said, "Yes, we find six to ten bodies a year, but Phoenix is not the murder capital of the United States." The canal had been empty for two weeks when I made my foray, so I had missed the good stuff, but it was still an opportunity to test my notion.

I was first overcome by the stench. It had rained in the night and the canal had a stagnant marine smell, as if the sea had been locked in a closet. The name of the original canal company—Swilling—floated to mind. The bottom was not the smooth surface I expected; rocky here and muddy there, it was grained with what looked like tide ripples between patches of standing water. Tiny clam shells nestled between bits of broken mirror, hubcaps, and plastic bags. The canal banks had the look of plain dirt, with weeds at the waterline, so that I was unsure whether I was looking at disintegrating gunite or a stretch of canal that had never been lined at all. As I forced myself to continue through what seemed a festering hospital corridor, I could see by the prints of people and dogs and the treads of bicycles that many adventurers had preceded me. Dominating all other refuse, the principal landmarks of that anticlimactic stroll, were shopping carts sprawling on their sides, on their ends, even upside down, at regular intervals. Dripping with algae that bleached like Spanish moss, stuck with shredded plastic, flecked with styrofoam, they loomed in that shrunken perspective with the grandeur of shipwrecks.

Just when my nostrils had reached their limit, my eye was caught by a frantic, swarming movement on the canal bottom in the distance. I raised the binoculars I carry in the most unpromising locales and found, to my astonishment, a flock of Audubon's warblers—the first I'd seen in metropolitan Phoenix—hopping, darting, veering off and back, stabbing greedily at nourishment I couldn't imagine. That banquet was the image that stuck when I tried to get to the bottom of Phoenix: the hunger of creatures, gorgeous in the individual, feeding in the most straitened circumstance.

The Face in the Canyon Wall

"See that face in the cliff?" repeats the person you are hiking with.

"No," you snap.

"It's as plain as your own. Those two little caves are the eyes, and the right one is a little higher than the left. That reddish shaft of rock is the nose, and the little ledge it's standing on is the mouth. Once you see it, it's obvious. It really looks mean. How can you *not* see it?"

Simple: you stare at the lupine by your feet. When you finally raise your eyes out of politeness, it is a blurred glance to the side. You walk on, changing the subject, because once you see the unwanted face you will never unsee it, and a fine expanse of fractured rock will turn into a bad mural with a mean look.

Seeing things as they are not is unavoidable, and the illusions don't have to be human. At any time the marl may erupt into dobermans, teacups, lampshades, ravioli. But your face-finding friend is taking the main drainage by finding a stone man staring back. The human form, whole or piece-meal, snags our imagination like nothing else. We live in such constant human complication that even our inner dialogue, on a quiet hike, supplies us with companions we didn't invite. If those who refuse to pick out faces in the cliff get surly, they may be on vacation from the human image. The sandstone teacup is emotionally neutral; the face in the wall makes cold stone radiate the mood projected upon it. A whole cliff glowers or smiles.

Our language for the natural world is saturated with our anatomy. Necks, arms, elbows and fingers of land; the mountain's head, its shoulders, its skirt, its feet; the brow of the hill; the mouth of the cave, canyon, or river; cypress knees, brain coral; the eye of the storm; the teeth of the wind; tongues of lava; the face of the land; the navel of the world. The Sleeping Giant, Mummy Mountain, Old Baldy. The Tetons, French for breasts; Solomon's Peak, formerly Solomon's Prick. It all makes Mount Rushmore quite superfluous.

Cosmologies we consider primitive populated the heights with humanized gods, but the most simple-minded did not pin their theology on dry resemblance. Mountains, rivers, the wind, sea and sky, were sources of power that shaped men's lives, sustaining them or wiping them out. But the mask of Pele did not *look* like the volcano where the goddess resided; the promontories sacred to Athena did not bear her profile. Certainly nothing in the earlier pantheon is so literal as the anthropomorphism expressed today at Franconia Notch, New Hampshire, where a formation shaped like a man's head, known as the Old Man of the Mountain, hangs from a cliff 1,200 feet in the air. For the last seventy years, eighteen steel pins have held the features in place, while the five-ton fore-head has been braced by a steel rod, lest erosion destroy what erosion blindly created. Route 93, part of the Interstate system, squeezes from four lanes to two through the fifteen miles

of Franconia Notch, partly for fear of potential damage to the
Old Man from the vibrations of construction.

"So it was now as they sought that state of prehistoric happiness which, by human beings, can only be imagined in terms
of a landscape bearing resemblance to the human body,"
wrote W. H. Auden in *The Age of Anxiety*. The figure in the
state of prehistoric happiness who went around identifying
things was, in our Judeo-Christian tradition, none other than
Adam in Eden. And it is at least teasing that the Judeo part of
our tradition actually has a mystic strain, centered on Adam,
that can justify the Old World's discovery of the face in the
New World cliff. It is called the Cabala.

Or it is the Kabbalah, or the Qabbala, or a dozen exotic
variants, and it is a strain of Jewish mysticism that surfaced
in Spain in the twelfth century. Transmitted as secret lore
from generation to generation of Hebrew scholars, the Cabala
claims to trace itself to Moses, who picked it up in Egypt and
secretly encoded it in the first four books of the Bible. The
Egyptians, in turn, had gleaned it from Abraham when he
was in Egypt, and Abraham inherited it through the patri-
archs from Adam—who received it from some visiting angels.
The Cabala, then, is a sacred oral tradition, as well as a collection of abstruse Hebrew writings that trace their secrets
beyond Adam to the messengers of Jehovah. Contradictory,
multi-faceted, the Cabala probably hides as many faces as
fractured shale.

One image, however, might be considered a text for those
who see in nature endless projections of the human person.
According to one of the Cabala's creation myths, the universe
began as a great primordial man, Adam Qadmon, a single
emanation of God's light. Because the universe required sepa-
rated matter and differentiated creatures, the first man broke
into lesser countenances, each revealing a separate aspect of
God. As creation continued through the process of disunion,
the countenances split and splintered, shrank and dissolved

into the universe of imperfection and variety we know today. Every piece of matter, then, is a remnant of an original, if symbolic, human being. The rock, the water, the dobermans, the ravioli are all split off the original Adam.

Adam Qadmon, of course, is a mystic representation of the familiar first man from Judeo-Christian and Islamic tradition. And it is Adam who, by naming the creatures, cast the web of language over the physical world. If creation began with the Word, it was Adam who refracted it into speech. Seeing the Adam of Genesis and Adam Qadmon as the popular and mystic facets of a single, diversified creation myth, one might say that Adam, in naming creation, was engaged in an act of self-recognition, of rediscovery. The universe was Adam in disguise, and in naming its parts, Adam was finding words for man's secret, disassembled self.

It is doubtful that any European explorers who tamed the Western Hemisphere with anatomical place names were practicing Cabalists—nor, I suspect, would any Cabalist on his way to enlightenment claim kinship with whoever named the Tetons or Old Baldy. But either by coincidence or by one of those connections that flashes light on the human interior, the person who delights in turning landscape into human beings has parodied the first step in what, for some, is a spiritual ascent. The meditator upon Adam Qadmon reverses the process of creation, progressing from multiplicity to unity, until he has reassembled our mythic ancestor. Beginning with individual, local manifestations of the man-in-the-world, the Cabalist works his way back through the divine emanations to the primal man of light—the original, mystic Adam—and beyond that to a final vision of the Creator. Our friend by the cliff, mimicking the first move, may not reach God; but by finding the world staring humanly back, he is on the brink of a mystic tradition.

If a detour into the Cabala proves nothing else, it shows that the relentless humanizing of everything around us has affinities with our central creation myth. And it is precisely that fixation on the human being that many who seek some interchange with the natural world today are trying to avoid. They see the human being neither as a starting point nor a culmination, but as a product of this moment in the unfolding of the universe. Standing in a semi-pagan tradition of American naturalists for whom turning to nature meant screening out man, they look with increasing desperation to the nonhuman for relief from our overpopulation and technology. Realists by intent, they wish to see rock as rock, trees as trees, the physical world in all its literal, hard-edged, multiple, unmetaphoric suchness. The last companion they want is a closet Cabalist finding mug shots in the cliff.

But to see the cliffs as geology and clouds as pure vapor takes focus amounting to a spiritual discipline of its own. Reality dislikes to be seen, and clear vision is ambushed with cumulus angels and stone toads. When someone points out the face in the wall, the enemy is not your companion but yourself, for the features, once seen, will not dissolve. The most antisocial among us bond with the human image. Whether the spoiler is mystic or garden variety, we are full of the old Adam.

Optic Nerve

We are constantly counseled not to lose sight of reality. "Keep your eyes open," goes the advice. "Bear witness," and, above all, "show your true colors." We realists are also great consumers of sunglasses, of tinted windshields, of bus windows that turn slums by the airport into romantic moonscapes. We arm ourselves with devices to bring reality up close, to stop it or let it flow on film. Shielding our eyes from each other with what we revealingly call shades, we cool the colors while retaining, socially, our cool. "Seeing is believing," we tell each other, then pay good money to change what we see.

Our fickleness is quite defensible, since the human claim actually to *see* reality can be dismissed in one skimmable paragraph. We never see objects themselves, only the waves that bounce off them from the electromagnetic spectrum. Of that profusion of wavelengths, we admit the pitifully thin band called visible light. The quantity of that band entering the eye is determined by the diameter of the pupil, as adjusted by the iris. It is focused on the way in by the cornea and falls on the millions of light receptors that compose the nerve tissue called the retina. The retina chemically transmits information along the optic nerve to the visual centers of the brain. There—crossing that inexplicable bridge between chemistry and perception, sense and sensibility, input and attitude—it is fashioned into what passes, for us, for fact.

The limitations of our eyeballs allow us to see like a man rather than, say, like a bird. The retina of the owl, for instance, has mostly receptors called rods, which have great light-gathering ability, poor resolution, and help to locate mice at night. The retinas of hawks are dense with cones, and they acutely focus resolution and color, and help to find mice at noon. Certain worms and anthropods have multiplex eye structures like facets of a jewel, and it is difficult to imagine *what* they see. Human beings are exceeded in the concentrations of both rods and cones by any other species—nor can we see, as some can, into the infrared or ultraviolet. It is only because our eyes, with middling abilities, are wired to that striking auxiliary, the human brain, that we can analyze light we don't see with spectrographs, augment it with telescopes, freeze it with cameras, and cool it with shades.

Attitudes toward visible reality seem part of the contradictory, changeable human personality, and fancy information about light waves and receptors has little impact on actual behavior. Aldous Huxley, who knew enough about vision to write a book about sharpening it, always traveled with three pairs of sunglasses, of varying tints, to "improve the landscape as well as soothe the eye." In northern Italy, which he faulted aesthetically for belonging neither to the north or the south, "the judicious traveler will don his green spectacles." Thus seen, Italy above Rome turns into a glorious northern landscape with the "seemingly luminous verdure of the English scene." My dim view of Huxley—that he breaks an essential bond with where he is by packing gear to transform it—

was put sorely to the test on a drive down the Baja Peninsula. As we passed Bahía Concepción, I remarked on the beauty of this desert fjord, plunging with sand and cactus to white crescent beaches, then out through shoals of aquamarine and turquoise to a bay of sapphire. "You should see it through polaroid glasses!" exclaimed my friend, handing them to me. To my astonishment, I could see many more levels of shoals, deeper in the water, each with an additional green shading into blue. The beaches remained white, the sky was darker, and the glasses had simply brought out flavors like a squeeze of lime. This was not Huxley turning Italy into England; this was amplifying the Mexico that was already there. My sense of unease—that by wearing polaroid glasses I was cheating on Bahía Concepción—was logically unsupportable.

Yet long after learning that the world is more or less dubbed by our senses, that one can alter light waves without sin, I have remained, perversely, a purist. Against warnings that I am courting cataracts and eye cancer, I don't wear sunglasses until blinding sand or snow shuts my eyes. I have tried, without success, to buy a car without tinted windows. I chucked out all the screens that came with the house: better an interior full of flies than a blurred view. And an urge to preserve the world in its imagined precision led to a thirty-year fascination with cameras that not only freeze the moment, but do so in stereo.

The gift of a View-Master, shortly after kindergarten, introduced the world in depth as a place to explore. A device whose variants are still on the market, the View-Master is a plastic viewer with two eye pieces, a slot for inserting a reel with fourteen tiny transparencies, and a lever to turn the reel. If you hold the viewer to the light, flick the lever, and peer, you are treated to seven scenic climaxes in three dimensions, as if at the end of a brief tunnel. I amassed a collection of over two hundred reels—more than 1,400 pictures—of such sights as

Mt. McKinley, Iguazu Falls, and the Sphinx. I felt as if I had *been* to these places. Arranging these reels alphabetically in the leather case of my father's broken movie camera, with a niche for the viewer, I could hold our whole scenic world, in color and 3-D, the way a businessman held a briefcase.

Seeing my stereoscopic bent, on my tenth birthday my parents gave me the most enchanting gift of my life—an artifact contemporaneous with but eclipsed in cultural history by the hula hoop—a Stereo Realist camera. To master the Stereo Realist was to grasp, intuitively, how our eyes reconstruct space. The camera takes two pictures at once, the same distance apart as the human eyes, and then the images are mounted on a single slide that slips into a viewer far more sophisticated than the View-Master. With a press of a button that lights the bulb behind the slide, the scene you have taken nearly leaps into your lap. Landscape lacks only sound and smell; you feel you could reach and touch it. People—in arrested motion or snapped indoors with a blinding flash—have more the reality of a wax museum.

The truth is that stereo, by capturing the three dimensions of space and abolishing that of time, often goes beyond reality—from realism to surrealism—and because the results seemed so convincing, I was ravished by them. Still water, seen with the naked eye, gains its liquidity by faintly trembling its reflections and turns to gelatin when that trembling is stopped in three dimensions. I took rolls of waterweeds in clear aspic. Water moving too fast to be stopped by the shutter turns to spun glass, and I shot a roll of Steuben waterfalls. I pried the slides open and reversed the transparencies, which exchanged near for far. Distant mountains loomed up front, cacti got larger as they receded, and a wrangler and mule tunneled like jigsaw cutouts to the horizon. I was at that unbearable age when the object of life is to do tricks that require observers—balancing on the eave on one leg while calling, "Hi, Mom!" making our spaniel jump through a hoop wound in tinsel—and the Stereo Realist was a ring in that circus. Looking back as a nominal adult on the few serious drug trips I attempted later, before I worried that unknown substances might permanently crosswire my eyes and brain, I realize that I never managed a true hallucination, never saw anything so interesting as that reversed stereo of a wrangler and mule shafting straight through the Superstition Mountains.

The stereo slide, as perfected in the fifties, has never been bettered as a medium for freezing the moment, and I tried to be its prodigy. My mother, an amateur watercolorist who survived the Depression doing furniture ads, taught me the rules of perspective and especially how to compose in the Stereo's nearly square frame. But the craze was brief and collapsed for social reasons. Party guests, exposed to new worlds or moments of their own pasts, gaped into the viewer and refused to pass it. The person with the slide would exclaim, "Imagine, Russell without wrinkles," or, "You won't believe the way Gladys wore her hair last fall," while others sat stonily, or scratched, or muttered, "Pass it on." Neighbors tried to break the impasse with a stereo projector so we could all see the same slide at once. Guests were forced into sophisticated versions of the cardboard glasses handed out at that tackier fifties phenomenon, 3-D movies. Projection lacked the fidelity of slides through a viewer, though I still remember a shot of a camel's frothing mouth that sailed right out of the screen and into the martinis.

Our family, with several stereoscopic branches, disdained projectors, but at reunions we all had to sit within reach of the viewer's cord or its extension. Romantics still gaped at the past, particularly when it starred themselves, while others, sick of snapping "Pass it on!" headed to the bar. We tried gathering around a table with a multiplicity of viewers. Slides came faster, but spectators were generally two or three shots behind what the photographer was describing. Viewers circled and cords braided until we were finally nose to nose at the center of the table, viewers in a knot. Patiently, we pulled the plugs, unbraided the cords, and broke out the next box of slides. Families like ours all over America were finding stereo photography antisocial, and gave up. An unconcerned loner, I kept clicking.

Because Kodak had sold its own stereo cameras during the heyday, they felt an initial obligation to keep mounting slides. Suddenly they slapped on an extra fee. Then they quit mounting slides altogether. You mounted slides yourself, or sent them to specialty outfits in places like Little Rock, Arkansas, or Gainesville, Florida. Stereo photography, once a family bond, became an abrasive, and the cameras, as if they knew it, stopped working. When I found a repairman who would condescend to work on one, it would take two rolls, then jam again. Well after college I tried converting to a conventional slide camera—thinking to combine marketable images with the words I was now producing—and emerge as a photojournalist. My mother's rules for composing in a square frame, which I had compounded with tricks for composing in depth, were valueless for pictures that were long, skinny, and flat. My senses rejected the new camera, and the results were even flatter than their medium. If the rage for preserving depth crested in the fifties, and was over, maybe the lesson was that the moment itself—irreplaceable as it was—shouldn't be kept.

It seems curious that someone too pure to wear sunglasses would switch from the surrealism of stereo slides to the amplification of binoculars, but tastes in hypocrisy mature. For years I thought binoculars were just for sporting events, or for bringing something close that you couldn't identify—was that cube in the distance a rock or a house? As for enhancing scenery, it actually dulled certain effects. By bringing you closer to mountains, for instance, it decreased the blue scattering of the atmosphere that gave them their wistful appeal, and if trained on peaks reddened by the slant rays of dawn

or sunset, it turned blush to ash. Since you were risking a
tangle with more than one strap around your neck, and hanging equipment was sure to collide mid-torso, cameras seemed
the millstone of choice. But my friends weren't identifying
distant cubes; they were watching birds.

I had gone through a year of birdwatching in late grade
school and ran through the suburban repertoire. In early
middle-age I joined my birding friends with cheap 7 × 35
binoculars. Whatever their setting, birds were compacted fire.
Lazuli buntings among desert willows were small combustions
of blue. Sun through the fanned-out tail of a red-tailed hawk
was pure carnelian against the sky. The gorgets of hummingbirds, the iridescence of grackles, the tucked yellow of drab
pine siskins were gradations of intensity. I was less interested
in species identification than my friends, more impressed by
the wavelengths that hit my retina, but the difference was
merely in emphasis. Just as once I seldom left home without
a stereo camera, now I endured binoculars.

Gradually, as I phased out film and phased in the amplified
eye, I realized I hadn't just switched appliances; I had changed
an attitude. I was augmenting the passing moment rather than
freezing it. Instead of keeping the three dimensions of space,
I was intensifying the fourth dimension of time. Suspiciously,
this focus on the fleeting moment occurred just as the finitude
of my own span on earth became more and more believable.
Time, I knew, looking forward, couldn't be kept, even on film.
The phrase, "You can't take it with you," coined for money,
applied equally to a trunk of stereos, that wax museum of
my youth. What descendant was going to go dizzy poring
over them all, assuming I bequeathed a functioning viewer?
As I started making trips with fellow birders—to Chiapas, to
Costa Rica, on the pretext of glimpsing that endangered, half-
mythical bird, the quetzal—our goal was to experience, within
the rondure of a lens, a single, dazzling, unrepeatable moment. No family members were going to gather at the round

table gaping at my feathered epiphany while relations-in-law snarled, "Pass it on."

Because of my tendency to lose and abuse equipment, I put off getting a pair of binoculars equal in quality to my childhood Stereo-Realist. But once committed to viewing the great solar eclipse of July 1991, at a dune camp south of La Paz, in Baja California Sur—in the shadow's center—I sprang for the finest, most expensive glasses I could find. It seemed fitting to inaugurate this splurge not with birds, but with solar flares from the very sun that illuminated them. The dune camp was, in fact, infested with a gamut of eclipse-chasing devices, including solar telescopes, that made my binoculars a mere toy, but I was not disappointed. Awaiting word that it was safe to look, then focusing on the blackened sun, I saw the spread wings of its solar flares, shot with strange purple filaments. I had initiated my binoculars with the ultimate bird. Wandering the dune top after the event, exchanging post-mortems with the sunstruck, I ran into a retired accountant I had met at breakfast. Around his neck was a leather case I couldn't believe. "Is that a Stereo-Realist?" I gasped.

"I wouldn't use any other camera," he replied.

Like someone unburdening a vice, I poured out the history of my experience with the Stereo-Realist, from preadolescent rush to adult withdrawal.

"But there's no need to give up stereo at all," he smiled. "There's a whole network of people who fix cameras and viewers, and mount slides. There are all kinds of groups who show each other their latest pictures. There are stereo clubs, a National Stereo Association, and there's a magazine called *Stereo World*. Stereo isn't anything you have to give up. It's something to enjoy for your entire life."

I was seriously shaken. Rather than being elated that I could solve my stereo problems, I was threatened. What I thought was a mature, if forced, decision about time itself was, in fact, ignorant, reversible. While I had no interest in joining clubs, I could still be a loner in lost worlds, and go back to freezing moments. When I finished talking to the accountant, I turned quickly seaward from that crowded dune. There was a formation of brown pelicans. As I brought them to focus, one of them folded its wings, plunged freefall, and fought its way back from water to air with a glistening fish. I was reassured, done with stopping motion. I was ready for life on the wing.

In all these contradictions, I like to think I have remained, as my stereo camera called itself, a Realist. Now that I carried binoculars to bring brilliance up close, I tried not to let the instrument take over. I had, for instance, ruined enough sunsets proving, again and again, that binoculars intensify colors at the source of light, in the west, while dulling their glow on mountains to the east. Yet there remained that whispering trickster, slipping into the moment between looking with the glasses and with the naked eye, making me wonder whether bringing the desert ranges up close really turned vermilion to ash or whether I was deceived by the shift in scale. Even as I relished watching faulted granite deepen from coral to plum, I spoiled the show by going back and forth.

It was on an evening that turned the blood of McDowell Peak to a heart of violet that I found the answer. I held the binoculars vertically so as to look through a single eyepiece. It took some positioning before I located the same formation with aided and unaided eyes, then superimposed the larger version on the smaller. The amplification wobbled, the peak in my naked eye stood still, and before me was the proof: an amethyst burning through a cloud of rose quartz. But I only found the solution by breaking with reality and making my binoculars, like my old stereo, do tricks.

It was in Baja California that my resolve to see the world plainly, through the naked eye, got one further comeuppance.

I was headed north from La Paz in a skiff, along the 120-mile
Sierra de la Giganta that crumbles into the Gulf of California
in ramparts of volcanic ash. I was anxious to memorize each
promontory, bay, and fishing camp of that roadless coast. The
vibration of the outboard and the salt of the wind weighted my
eyes, which came to rest on the racing, reflected, blinding sun.
I was hypnotized by waves in electric zigzags, a kind of neon
art. My eyelids sank farther, exhausted, half-drugged. The
zigzags bled vertically, ran together. I squinted painfully until
my eyes watered and the lines of light went haywire. When
my eyelids touched, I was shot inward into a huge, translucent
cave and was aware, with vision strangely reversed, of figures
of light dancing on a circular screen behind me.

It struck me that I had been plunged into a parody of one of
our earliest Western myths, the image of the cave in Plato's
Republic. Human beings, in Plato's parable, are seated in a
cave and chained so that they cannot turn their heads. A fire
burns behind them, a sort of puppet show takes place between the fire and their backs, and what they take to be the
world is merely a shadow play projected on the wall in front
of them. While Plato's parable has many meanings, some of
them moral, one of his points is that the world we take in, and
believe, is constructed—dubbed—by our senses. It is a truth
elaborated by two-and-a-half millennia of ensuing science.
If the cave-bound were suddenly hauled to the world above,
according to Plato's myth, they would at first be too dazzled
by the radiance to make it out. But eventually they would be
able to stare directly at the world illumined—and, for Plato,
caused—by the sun.

I opened my eyes and saw the sun's zigzags, closed my eyes,
and was back in the cave. I differed from Plato's chain-bound
only in that I saw the fire in back, not the shadow play in front.
Over and over I shot between overbright gulf and luminous
cave. Whatever the source of this recurring myth, it had the

restorative power of sleep. Shuttling back and forth, inside and out, brilliance to glow, gave me new eyes for the coast. Giving surrealism, irrationality, parable their due, I was ready to see these improbable mountains as they *were*. I was ready, at least, for the reality we evolved for.

The Light Brigade

"I've always wanted to camp in the desert with a view of city lights, and that's just what I'm doing here." The speaker was an apprentice architect giving a tour of Taliesin West, Frank Lloyd Wright's architectural school outside Phoenix. Perhaps he sensed a shiver in one of his listeners, for he went on to say, "Most of the old-timers here don't like the lights at all. The archivist thinks they're an abomination. But to me, they're not only beautiful, they also put me in touch with my future clients. Most people now want houses that look down on the city."

Did the shiver mean that I was ready for the archives myself?

Granted, parting the light from the darkness has been found good since Genesis 1:3. In its urban configuration, light reminds almost everyone who looks down on it of the same thing. "It's just like a jewelry store window." How can anyone complain of jewels on velvet?

One would have to be a crank to dismiss the great American skylines—Manhattan, Chicago from the lake, San Francisco spiring and spilling across its hills. Even as those cities are defaced by curtain-wall shafts and glass massifs, they retain the sense that chance, sculpting with building contracts, has composed a classical nighttime frieze. But if a city has enough elbowroom to grow out instead of growing up, as is particularly the case in the West, light never gets sculpted. The texture may vary as the amber of sulphur lights replaces the ice of mercury lights, as wattage intensifies around sports fields, and as traffic arteries clog with headlights and taillights. There may be a business corridor where high rises sprout in the runoff. But are the city's jewels ever laid out like constellations—the hunter, the dipper, the crab—or in spiral nebulae, or in Magellanic clouds? No; the city is the rectangle squared, block upon block, until geology or economics cuts it off. Look down on a town and it could be any town. Always the same rhinestones, the same baubles, the same paste laid out in the same deadening crosshatch, and no one ever fires the window dresser.

If light were not parted so elegantly from the darkness overhead, one might be more grateful for the grosser effects below. But the coagulation of urban lights seals the sky, blotting the hunter, the dipper, the crab. So fixed is the penumbra that at any hour of the night, moon or none, one can hike the mile-long trail up Phoenix's Squaw Peak, gaining 1,000 feet over switchbacks and granite scrambles, simply by following the luminous beaten path. That eclipse of the stars is more than an aesthetic problem in the Southwest, where astronomy, remote as it may seem, is big business. Astronomers from Kitt Peak and other telescope rookeries have complained bitterly about the interference of light within the visual range. The 100-inch telescope at Mt. Wilson Observatory, near Los Angeles, has already been closed because of light pollution. The night sky over Palomar Mountain, 50 miles northwest of San Diego, is

100 percent brighter than natural background—which turns the United States's largest optical telescope into what is, in light-gathering ability, a diminished instrument.

The sky over the National Observatory at Kitt Peak, 55 miles southwest of Tucson, is only 6.5 percent brighter than it would be naturally, but the threat has been sufficient to lead astronomer David Crawford to found the International Dark-Sky Association, which he describes as a kind of "nighttime Sierra Club." Dark-Sky describes its enemies with connoisseurship. "Glare" is "bright, troublesome, uncomfortable," contributes to nighttime accidents, and is sufficiently addictive that some people think there is no illumination at all unless glare is present. "Light trespass" invades your territory, ruins your eyes' adaptation to dark, and can spark neighborhood squabbles. "Clutter" is "trashy light," a "visual litter" that confuses more than it informs. "Urban sky glow" is the collective stray light of cities that replaces the heavens. And the lyrically named "veiling luminance" is light so bright it actually obscures what it tries to reveal.

The Dark-Sky Association may have been founded by astronomers protecting their profession, but it addresses concerns of the general public, including the waste and expense of unneeded light. Dr. Crawford estimates that the average homeowner pays an additional $5 to $10 a month for wasted rays, and that the nation as a whole adds roughly $1 billion to its annual light bill. Some lights, claims Dr. Crawford, use up to one hundred times the current needed for the task. The energy to create light comes from the combustion of fossil fuels and to a lesser degree from hydroelectric power and the split atom. Light pollution thus contributes to other pollutions such as acid rain, global warming, dammed rivers, and nuclear waste. Light, most glaringly squandered in cities, runs on energy cabled in from rural areas that are treated like colonies.

Once light pollution is recognized, remedies are cheap and

abundant. Street and parking lights need only illuminate what's below and can be capped with shields. If billboards must be seen at night—rather than, say, torn down—they can be lit from the top down rather than from the bottom up. Lights that burn at the wrong hour can be rigged with timers. Some of the worst technologies are on the way out, including bulbs and globes that work by filament, producing more heat than light, and mercury lamps—those ghastly blue tubes— which produce ultraviolet light we can't see. Both can be replaced with low-pressure sodium lights, Dark-Sky's favorite. Sodium light is the pinkish amber of ripe papaya and can illuminate public spaces on as little energy as ten watts per tube.

Leading the forces of darkness, Dr. Crawford has prevailed upon communities in the Southwest to include such changes in new lighting codes. All of Arizona's counties and its major cities now have astronomer-approved ordinances. An updated lighting system at an Arizona prison has improved security and reduced light pollution while cutting costs in half. And by converting its street lights to low-pressure sodium, the city of San Diego saves roughly $3 million a year on its light bill while actually increasing the number of lights.

Faster than towns can be doused, however, we are spraying light in all directions, and not just because we want to light up rooms, traffic corridors, and ballparks. More and more, it seems, we are turning night into day in an attempt to "make the streets safe," in hopes that a few photons will fall into the urban cracks, flushing out the slasher, the rapist, the assassin. The net effect of such zeal is to create areas of brilliance next to holes of deep shadow that are perfect for the very attackers we are trying to discourage. Deprived of our night vision by the glare, lulled by mock daylight, we may not see mischief springing toward us through the veiling luminance. Dark-Sky doesn't discourage public lighting for safety, but recommends a modest glow that eliminates strong transitions from light to dark. For those who feel threatened in their own quarters, better than the spotlight that trespasses on your neighbor is the infrared sensor, which only switches on when it detects movement.

Such, then, is the changing scene that the fan of city lights wishes to look down on from his well-designed window. As Dr. Crawford points out, dimming the lights so we can see the stars puts us back in touch with the universe that spawned us, and to which we still belong. Light coming out of darkness may be beautiful regardless of the use to which it is put, and perhaps one shouldn't go into a moral spasm because a tour guide likes to camp over lit-up towns. But sensibilities have surely shifted when an apprentice to America's foremost architecture, heir to a tradition of building to blend with nature, would rather align himself with man's light than with the starry universe, and looks forward to obliging clients who wish to share that view in something less modest than a tent.

Outside the astronomy community, the taste for darkness is dying of unfamiliarity, and only old-timers remember the nighttime desert as Frank Lloyd Wright described it—as the floor of a vast ocean, with the staghorn cactus as coral and man at the edge of an exhilarating abyss. When power lines prepared to bisect his property, hauling more light to Phoenix, Wright threatened, in vain, to burn his creation down. Before light won, it was surely delicious for him to stand at the prow of the great stone and canvas ship that was his Taliesin, gaze into a void that was not yet Scottsdale, and imagine himself steering builders of the future between the blackout and the stars.

Roots

We had converged again—Karen, the caretaker, and Remo and I, the guests—for Thanksgiving at the little ranch nestled into a fold of Utah sandstone. Two Thanksgivings back, during a day hike, we had watched a stag deer fall toward us from a three-hundred foot cliff. The Thanksgiving after that we let a cowboy neighbor leave schwacked on peppermint schnappes, and the next morning found sidewinder tread-marks in the snowy drive. This year Remo arrived with his right hand bandaged from an operation for carpal tunnel syndrome and Karen was at the end of her caretaking duties. This looked to be the last of our trio of ranch Thanksgivings, and we were in the mood for a quiet, reflective, even unmemorable time.

I pulled in the night before, just after sundown. A fire was warming the hot tub—the ranch's one nod to indulgence—and corned beef and cabbage was brewing on the stove. It was a dish I hadn't had in years, and the homey reek took me back to childhood. Soon it was in our bowls, framed by candles and white jug wine. Remo, mashing his vegetables, remarked that one of them seemed quite tough.

"I forgot to warn you," laughed Karen. "I put in some horse-radish roots to flavor it, but you weren't actually supposed to eat them. No harm if they're not too hot."

I didn't notice any spice, just pure nostalgic flavor, and I joined the others in a huge helping of seconds. In the middle of recounting a recent trip to Denver, my eyelids suddenly felt heavy, as if I had spent the day in a fierce wind. Then my eyes stopped working as a team and the formation of each sentence became a challenge. I felt embarrassed to feel so unfocused by the second glass of wine, calculated my speech beforehand, and hoped no one would notice. After dinner I offered to wash dishes. "You can't because you're last to arrive, and Remo can't because of his hand," said Karen. "Go join him in the living room by the fire."

In a couple of minutes Karen followed me to the living room to remark that her mouth was irrationally dry. "I'm thirsty, too," I said, "but corned beef *is* salty." After a glass of water I rejoined Remo. He asked a question about Denver, and in the middle of my answer his head slumped to his chest: he was asleep. I went to inform Karen and found her sacked out in the bedroom. As I stood in bafflement, Remo appeared, saying, "I want to lie down for a bit."

Karen opened her eyes and said, "Something has hit us. Maybe we can sleep for a couple of hours and still go in the hot tub. Maybe the wine was bad."

"What was in the corned beef?" asked Remo.

"Just the stuff you could see," said Karen, "plus the horse-radish and some juniper berries I bought in town, for flavoring."

I left the propane light on over my bed in the living room

for another three hours, dozed, then read, forcing my eyes to
track. I still wanted to luxuriate in hot water, surrounded by
sandstone and stars, and I hoped that our party would rally.
At last I flipped off the propane and the room went opaque.

At three in the morning, the outside door near my bed burst
open and a light shot into my face. "Oh, sorry," said Remo,
wielding a flashlight. "I was having trouble breathing and
went outside to walk."

"Is there something I can do?" I said. "Are you going to be
okay?"

"I'll be all right," he muttered, and passed through the
house to the bedroom.

I woke at dawn, made coffee, and waited two hours for the
others to get up. Karen stumbled out first. "Remo was certainly weird last night," she said. "When I came back from
the bathroom, he said, 'Who was that woman who was just
lying next to me?' meaning me. He got up four times to walk
in the night. He said we should be quiet so we don't wake
the French family, who left a month ago. He also said he was
afraid he had awakened Ken."

"That was me," I said.

"Not that I'm a great judge of things," continued Karen. "I
couldn't walk straight or form coherent sentences."

"At least I feel normal."

"Have you looked at your eyes in the mirror?"

I went into the bathroom to find my pupils dilated as if by
belladonna.

At last Remo emerged and began recounting his night. He
had gone outside four times to walk and had fallen twice.
On the bench by the hot tub he saw a small girl wrapped
in a green towel, but something distracted him and when he
looked back she was gone. Several times he lost the thread
and asked, "What was I just saying?" The worst, he said, was
that when he was in the bathroom reaching down for a Klee-

nex, the nail clippers slipped out of his pocket and into the john, and he retrieved them with his bandaged hand.

"You put your operated hand into the *toilet?*" I gasped.

"Fraid so."

When Remo finished his recitation and Karen left to feed the horses, Remo asked, "Have I shown you the paintings on the bedroom ceiling?"

I couldn't remember any paintings, but I had never really focused on the bedroom décor and I followed. To me the ceiling was pure white, with the impasto of bad plastering. "What do you see?" I asked.

As if I were blind, he replied, "The tepees and Indians and mountains."

"Where are the mountains?"

Remo waved his bandaged hand along an edge of plasterboard.

"Show me a tepee."

Remo looked hard, then gestured toward a chance isoceles triangle of plaster. I could see that one could dream a landscape into the mottled ceiling, as one could with stains in wallpaper, but Remo was seeing something more Sistine. When Karen came back from the corral, I overheard Remo say, "I just showed Bruce the painting on the ceiling of the cars falling into the pit."

With dinner guests due, Karen had planned to start preparations at dawn and finally got started early afternoon. We finished last night's still unwashed dishes, chopped, crammed stuffing into the bird, and cooking was underway. Midafternoon, to our relief, Remo announced that he, too, now saw only plaster on the bedroom ceiling. I kept peering into the bedroom mirror and found my pupils dark and luminous. After five, our three guests—a cowboy, an architect, and a state park ranger—showed up at the same time, and we regaled them with the night's adventures. "Just what was in the meal?" asked the park ranger.

Karen, rehearsing the ingredients, suddenly put her hand to her cheek and said, "Oh, my god."

"What?" we said, nearly in unison.

"When the French family was here, they wanted to work in the garden. I didn't want them messing with a system they really didn't understand, so I asked them to pick some vegetables. I also told them they could dig up some horseradish roots and told them where they were. I forgot that the horseradish was growing in the middle of the datura. The jimson weed!"

I laughed even as I felt myself run cold, recalling Castaneda books from the seventies in which sorcerer Don Juan prepares poisonous, psychotropic datura to transport the author and, with him, the reader. Sacred datura jokes and cracks about separate realities were staples of our desert trips. Now, twenty years later, datura had taken its revenge.

"Let me see the root," said the ranger.

Karen brought out a pale, knobby tuber. The ranger took it and said, "It doesn't look like horseradish." She licked the cut end, rashly I thought, and said, "It doesn't taste like horseradish either."

The poison-plant book back home identified our spice as *Datura metaloides*, also known as *Datura inoxia* and *Belladonna de pobre*, or poor man's belladonna. Its lore is treated at some length in *The Marriage of the Sun and Moon*, by Andrew Weil. "*Datura* is not a nice drug," writes Dr. Weil. Its pharmacologic effects are caused by chemicals called tropane alkaloids, which block neurotransmission in the parasympathetic nervous system. Symptoms include "rapid heart rate; dilated pupils; flushing, warmth, and dryness of skin; dryness of the mouth"; and, in toxic quantities, "fever, delirium, convulsions, and collapse. Death may occur." Its shamanistic use is infrequent because there is no way to control its effects, though it is sometimes served maliciously by "poisoners, criminals, and black magicians." I managed to reach

Dr. Weil by phone. We were lucky, he said, in that the root was the plant's least toxic part, but no amount of cooking would reduce the alkaloids. He ends his *Datura* chapter rather charmingly by saying that he occasionally follows a Colombian custom of laying *Datura* flowers on his pillow to induce vivid dreams. But flower sniffing is the closest contact Dr. Weil cares for.

With that gastronomic flourish we ended our Thanksgivings at the ranch. We would miss the suicidal deer, the wranglers on schnappes, the psychotropic corned beef, but perhaps it was time to join our respective relatives for the traditional urban turkey.

Comfort That
Does Not Comprehend

People growing older are said to return to the moods and culture of their origins, if not its actual place. I can't imagine returning to the moods of suburban Chicago, an origin I never even revisit. I feel that I sank my first earthly roots when I arrived at the Sonoran desert outside Phoenix, at the age of eight. My family revisited it frequently during my childhood, and fate collaborated in my adult return. A number of years after my father died of the asthma that sent us to Arizona in the first place, my mother married a Chicagoan with a house outside Phoenix—to which they moved. I began visiting my mother and Frank over Christmas holidays. Then, when Frank acquired larger quarters—large enough for radically different people to live compatible lives—I started joining him and my mother for entire winters, lingering into spring. In my thirties I had managed to reproduce my season of discovery at the age of eight: I was living in the Sonoran desert, five miles from where I first saw it.

The area was unusual for Phoenix, with the city's tradition of bulldozing the desert and replacing cactus with plants from back East, or California, or Australia, without questioning whether they look right, guzzle water, or spread allergies. This particular neighborhood's pioneers zoned for five-acre parcels, with a premium on keeping the desert intact. In practice, they didn't let the cactus get too close to their living quarters, and in the case of Frank's purchase, the desert in front was fended off by a wall of oleanders surrounding a parking area, so that from my bedroom I looked out on gravel, then impenetrable leaves, then the gray slag of Mummy Mountain. In back, the requisite pool was blockaded by citrus, cassia, fig, laurel, and loquat, punctuated by two date palms. The landscaper had effectively partitioned the property, with the desert on the outside and man in the middle. Such arrangements gave humanity a desert setting rather than a desert life, but most plant and bird species, rabbits, and the inventive coyote withstood the holders of title insurance.

Because this new place was, in its minor way, a spread, it had live-in maintenance in the form of José, an aging Mexican whom Frank had employed since he first owned property in Arizona. A slow-moving man who stood with a hose to nonnative plants, José clipped when shagginess got flagrant and nursed his diabetes in a folding chair in the sun. I came and went, taking it upon myself, uninvited, to defend the property's desert, which needed only to be left alone. A guest of the interior, I found myself passing through the oleander curtain like a defector, rooting for what didn't need my help.

Winters that blurred without incident were rudely interrupted: Frank died after being assaulted by a stranger. Shortly thereafter, José entered the V.A. hospital with terminal diabetes: bonded for nearly a quarter of a century, he and Frank had almost departed together. The spread, bought by Frank alone, would ultimately go to his heirs but was my mother's to occupy while she survived. In the room vacated by José she installed a Vietnam veteran whose chief interests in life were studying electronics, reading the Bible, and pulling weeds. One day, in a panic, I stopped him from tidying the exterior desert because he thought that native plants, being small, numerous, and anonymous, were weeds. After three years of tending plants in return for a room, the veteran got his electronics degree and left. That was the end of live-ins. From this point on, the property was managed by a gardening crew that showed up one morning a week. My mother inhabited the spread alone until I appeared at Christmastime and realized that the cactus outside the oleanders needed a more active defense.

The desert, of course, has a natural attrition rate that it was my privilege to watch. The oldest saguaro on the property, baroque in its profusion of arms, had an eye-level window where the pulp had rotted away from the ribs, showing how they hold the cactus up like rebar. Inflicting my cactus lecture on occasional visitors, I could demonstrate how saguaros branched, how woodpeckers gouged holes that cauterized into homey caves for other species—too frequently, now, invader starlings—then lead the poor guest (mind the cholla!) to the demonstration cutaway model. "And this is how saguaros are built. . . ." The inset was only a few inches in each direction, a bit of desert intaglio, vaguely lyre-shaped, with ribs for strings.

Having seen saguaros survive all manner of accidents and assaults, I saw no threat in the little hole, but the first thing I noticed on returning to Phoenix one December was that the whole candelabra was tilting from that spot. Immediately I knew the cactus was doomed. With every rain the pulp takes in as much water as possible, its ribs expanding like bellows. At the first downpour this one would draw water to its many limbs above the weak point and come crashing down. Judging by the height, it would hit part of the driveway, flattening anything beneath. But the chance of its finding anything to flatten was infinitesimal, and in any case, what a memorable obituary. Out of curiosity I even gave it a little push, carefully, through the needles, just above the lyre. I was about as effective as the time I tried the same thing on the Tower of Pisa.

Too quickly I became used to the new shape and didn't even think about the saguaro on a night of pummeling wind and rain, the first winter storm. The next morning I bundled up to retrieve the paper—Arizona was impeaching the hilarious Governor Mecham and I lived for each installment. Halfway out the drive I stopped in my tracks: several tons of highly structured pulp lay at my feet. The rest of the cactus dipped through a small arroyo and rose toward the drive. Here and there, little breaks in the skin showed fresher green. The tip extended two feet over the asphalt. Slightly below it, like a snapped neck, lay a major fracture. I had estimated the saguaro's age to be close to two hundred years, and there was comfort in knowing that—unlike most of Phoenix's recently fallen saguaros—this one had died a quite natural death. The part of me that gave it a push was also sorry not to have watched it go.

Upright, it appeared serene; prostrate it seemed to writhe. The woodpecker holes facing the sky had filled with water and had become, unexpectedly, miniature potholes. I dipped my finger; the water was icy. I had never walked a fresh saguaro and tried this one: the smooth trunk was a pliant log while the needled branches crackled like a stubble field. Doomed as this saguaro may have been, one of its limbs had put forth a new branch no bigger than a tennis ball. A tight formation, it had landed with its arms side by side like basking crocodiles.

The tip in the drive would have to be dealt with. I tried kicking the cactus aside, but it was firmly attached. I returned with a saw, expecting minor resistance, but the ribs and pulp gave way like pound cake and the tip proved light enough to shove with my foot into the arroyo. As far as I was concerned, that was full clean-up. Most particularly I didn't want that year's gardening crew, looking for inventive chores once they had watered the loquat and trimmed the cassia, to suggest removing the corpus at an hourly rate. It was not practical to explain the weird urge to watch cactus pulp decay, but even professional gardeners understood that the tough woodpecker holes, once freed from the cactus, became "cactus boots." Suitably lacquered, cactus boots were sold in Scottsdale souvenir shops. When the gardeners paid their weekly call, I told them to ignore the dead saguaro. "I want to save the boots."

Natural attrition was outpaced, alas, by human inadvertence plus the notion that the desert was a 360-degree corridor for human support systems. The children next door, for instance, built a treehouse in a paloverde they thought was on their property. They played fort for a season, then the boards fell into an arroyo. The punctured tree turned sallow, then gray, then tumbled into the arroyo next to the fallen treehouse, intact to the last twig, looking like an upended root system. One morning the children's father appeared at the door to ask if he could take a truck to his side yard from our driveway to haul out some citrus trimmings. My mother, caught in a bathrobe and without make-up by a neighbor she was meeting for the first time, said certainly: anything to abbreviate the conversation. The truck mangled creosote bushes, dug permanent tracks, and after it left I piled a barrier of stones so no one would take its path for a spur. The same year, on the other side of the house, the septic tank rudely announced that it had filled, and it had to be dug up and replaced. The disemboweling spread baked clay over an area in which not the least weed subsequently took root.

Whatever its beatings, the desert remained lush enough to crowd the public road by the house, and it seemed appropriate that desert pavement—that slightly blackened mosaic of weathered stones, lichen, and small weeds set tight—met real pavement. But the phone company needed to lay line parallel to the road. Here my mother and I became aware of our frail grip on the place, for it was technically owned by Frank's estate and managed by a bank, and we could only watch as a phone company foreman promised a bank representative that the cable crew would respect the desert and revegetate anything they disturbed. They made a surgical cut three feet deep and four inches wide. I was impressed too soon, for next they brought in a back hoe, gouged a trench around the cut, and masticated a fifteen-foot strip. Desert pavement that met asphalt had been milled into red earth, raw rocks, and chewed plants. Could a utility crew actually revegetate lichen and bursage, and simulate the tiny, anonymous growth that makes the desert look authentic even to someone who doesn't know its particulars?

The bank next learned that the phone company had put the line in the wrong place, but now that it was installed they wanted to leave it and dedicate it as a general utility line. The bank objected, rightly, that it would be exhumed for gas lines and TV cables as soon as it was revegetated, and sued to have the phone company move it where their right-of-way ran— under the road. A compromise was struck whereby the phone company could leave it where it was, had sole use, and had to make good on the revegetation. When I returned the next fall, all I saw was red earth, and I assumed there had been no attempt at all. A month later I stumbled across six clusters of dead twigs in tiny craters: revegetation had consisted of six bursage planted midsummer, watered once, and left to die. Under court order from the bank, the phone company at last hired a nursery to install sixty-three plants—bursage, brittle-bush, and jojoba—in simulated randomness throughout the red strip, and to water them for a year.

Because of such blows, each time I returned to my mother's house I toured the property in trepidation before I unpacked the car. Had a utility retrenched? Did the dead saguaro survive? Above all, had anyone felled the desert willow? Preserving the willow had become a preoccupation. Native to higher elevations and installed by the previous owners in a garden in back, the desert willow, in late spring, was the property's most beautiful sight, all grace and lacework, a spill of ferny leaves and pale orchidlike blooms. Because it kept the rhythm of its habitat, losing its leaves in October and withholding them until May, I had to explain to each gardening crew that it was not, in fact, a dead tree. One year I returned to find it had been hacked until it looked like an angst-ridden prop from *Waiting for Godot*, and its next attempt to flourish looked more like seaweed on a piling. The gardening crew had remembered my words, knew it was a live tree but trimmed it back because when it leafed out it would cast too much shade on the petunias they planned to install. Such was the folly of sinking my own roots where they had so little purchase.

On the other hand, the desert exhilarated through sheer surprise. Once I stepped out for the morning paper, anticipating more on the gubernatorial recall, and found the first light wrapped in a cold fog through which burned a moon just past full. Two Harris' hawks broke dark and huge into the sky and lit on the tops of nearby saguaros. A third hawk lit on the mailbox like news of disaster. All, including my footsteps, froze, the visible shrunk to this tight tableau while sound, as if through far speakers, reported the roar of commuters on their way into Phoenix. Another dawn I heard, just past the oleanders, the rustle of water. The property's arroyo, which never flowed except in the frenzy of a downpour, was running a clear sweet stream. I followed uphill through neighboring yards to the road, where I found a city truck and two men in jeans: a water main had burst.

"Leave it," I said. "It's great."

"It won't be so great when you turn on the shower and there's nothing there."

"I'll bathe in the stream."

"Not if you want to stay healthy."

This diversion may have further lowered the aquifer under our neighborhood, but it was a pleasure to see water evading its fate in toilets and swimming pools.

The good news was that the desert reinvented itself, endlessly. Clumps of prickly pear would die in the middle and spread at the edge like supernovae. Imported species like cow's tongue prickly pear, from Texas, could be seen claiming arroyos. Creative in its ploys was a smooth-padded prickly pear import, ten feet tall, that had been struck by frost. Dropped pads by the dozens curled beneath it like old snapshots. A few turned into shallow cups that sent a taproot from the middle of the pad straight into the soil. The largest surviving branch of pads leaned over so far it touched the ground, rerooted itself, and sent up a fresh branch like the tail on a check mark. The central pad in the arch of pads, its capstone, was dry as parchment, so that parent and offspring were joined by a link that had actually died.

Just past the oleanders a century plant, which takes a quarter of that time to flower and die, had sent up a twenty-foot stalk. Instead of keeling over, the dead stalk remained upright the following year and turned into a popular bird perch. At last something of the desert could be seen over the oleanders from my bedroom window, and my visitors' count included doves, thrashers, woodpeckers, finches, quail, a cardinal, a kestrel. One night this spindle held a dark star at the top. I got the binoculars to make sure and sharpened the ear tufts of a great horned owl.

The most curious adaptation took place at the site of an old stable in back, torn down when a building inspector complained to my mother about its flapping aluminum roof. After the cement and bare ground beneath it were revealed, I kept my eye on the spot to see what would take root. Nothing, in fact, did take root, any more than it did over the emptied cesspool. Paloverdes still swayed to avoid a roof no longer there, a prickly pear dropped the pads yellowed in the stable's shade, and the cement floor stored the sun's heat. What turned out to be worth watching was the stable's one remaining fixture, a faucet that rose twenty inches from the ground and made a U-turn to a spigot that still poured a full stream when opened. Shut tight, it leaked a large drop of water every few seconds. This water did not vanish into desert air but filled a vessel that someone had placed beneath it years—perhaps decades—back. Fourteen inches long, eleven inches wide, seven inches deep and bright turquoise, this container was filled to the brim in all weather with a variable green murk. Along the top of one side ran a silver bar that said, in tall elegant letters, VEGETABLE CRISPER.

Source of water for the previous owner's horses, this faucet may have doubled as a wildlife oasis ever since a receptacle was placed beneath it, and removal of the barn around it may have only revealed its function. I laid a foam pad behind the paloverdes, which provided a screen, and watched the succession. Ground squirrels stretched on their hind feet and lowered their heads over the rim. Doves, harbingers of water to the desert traveler, perched on the rim and drank, as did finches and those Brits run amok, the starling and the English sparrow. Mockingbirds arrived in pairs, one leading the other, scattering whatever was there first.

Acrobatic types preferred the faucet to the bin. Hornets hovered around the mouth until the arrival of a Gila woodpecker, which perched on the side of the pipe and twisted its bill upward. Facing greater contortions was the curve-billed thrasher, whose bill curves downward, and which had to revolve its neck so that the bill, in fact, curved upward into the falling drop. Perched on this strange metallic tree, birds waited as each fruit ripened, swelling into a globe that, up

close, could be seen to catch the saguaros and paloverdes upside down in a tiny jewel. As a drop lost its grip and fell into
a bird's bill, cactus and all, the next drop began to swell.

It was, I suppose, an odd household—a woman in her seventies living alone in a rambling house obscured by vegetation in
a suburbanized desert, joined seasonally by an adult son who
fretted about all that couldn't be seen from the house—divid-
ing their responsibility for property that belonged, legally, to
neither of them. My mother, having outlasted two older husbands, at last acquired a younger boyfriend, a jet pilot, who
often stayed with us. When she suddenly lost him as well, to
cancer, she realized she would no longer have what she called
a "beau." "Your mother's a black widow," said an audacious
friend. It wasn't that; it was that the line she came from—
Landers and Kenworthys of whom I learned little because my
mother wasn't interested in family history—had a hard time
getting born, but once they existed they were practically un-
killable. Relatives of my mother's that I met as a child were
already old, had one aging offspring apiece, or none, or didn't
marry, but lived into their eighties and nineties. I became my
mother's only living blood relative, and while the Berger side
reproduced in moderation, I was pleased to be a dead-end
Lander or Kenworthy. Given our probable longevity, we could
look forward to an infinity of winters in which she pursued
golf and I explored the desert. Our interests coincided more
closely when she was painting deft watercolors of the landscape I loved, but those were times when she was tending
sick husbands, or a sick boyfriend, and art was her only out-
let. While there was no injunction against conversing in the
house, curiously, we only talked seriously when we were off
the property—exploring the new restaurants that purported
to have invented something called Southwestern cuisine.

So it was that as the water gathered and fell from the faucet
by the vanished stable, each drop holding the world upside

down, then letting go, that my mother's heart unaccountably stopped beating. She was only eighty and had been planning to fly alone to Greece in the spring. The ten days in the hospital between the first symptoms and the end were, in the leisurely rhythm of our lives, an instant. I had been planning to stay another four months, and the heirs and the bank allowed me those months "to wind things up." In the aftermath of this inscrutable event, its vacuum, I passed through the oleanders, scotch or coffee in hand, into the desert that now seemed so worn by our presence. How strange it seemed to have arrived as a guest, become a migrant, seen the passing of Frank, of José, of my mother, to be a tenancy's last, and temporary, survivor. From behind the paloverdes I watched doves drink from the crisper, saw the thrasher contort on the faucet, heard the mockingbird peal insolently as ever. Since the property had lost, for me, its human core, it seemed eerie to watch the continuity of it, the sheer sense that nothing had happened.

Because the house now passed to Frank's heirs, two middle-aged daughters from the Midwest who had no intention of moving into it, a FOR SALE sign was swiftly hammered next to the mailbox, with one of the bank's tentacles serving as realtor. Hedges and flower beds were to be maintained for prospective buyers and the desert, as usual, to be ignored. The bank knew its market, for the few prospects scrutinized the oasis in the middle and only asked about the acreage. There was speculation on the bank's part that the house, adequate in its day, was quite obsolete with its low ceilings and rambling floor plan, and a buyer might just want to knock it down and start over. I could only speculate what the razing of one house and the raising of another, more stylish, more fashionably bloated, would do to the crowd at the crisper.

But I had four months to empty the domain within the oleanders, the area I had slept in and ignored. Heaped in drawers, closets, and storage areas were two octogenarians' souvenirs of life. Frank's two daughters flew in from Illinois and Minnesota, lightened the load, and left. Bankers, lawyers, and realtors filtered through the disarray. Some of my mothers' possessions—clothing, accessories—could go to her friends, beyond which loomed an estate sale. More unwieldy were her letters, diaries, and more stereo slides than even I had taken. I looked until my eyes fused at the numberless duplicate cruises she took between husbands, with Frank, with her jet pilot, looked until I arrived at my childhood in three dimensions and stopped time. Last and least, I faced my own accretions. They were principally books, relieved by my collection of desert treasures in their bookshelf hollow, furred with dust. Into a burlap bag I had unlittered from the desert, I stashed the leghold trap, the tortoise shell, the pre-Columbia ceramic heads, the burned plate, the cactus boots and related booty, the true detritus of my winters in Phoenix, the desert in a sack.

During those four months I compulsively left doors and windows open, let anything that so desired crawl into the house. I set a card table outside and watched a new crop of cactus wrens explore my typewriter. I lay on the stable's cement floor and felt its stored heat pass through me into the night. One afternoon when I returned to the house, a small red and black snake slithered across the kitchen and into a little hole, previously unnoticed, under the carpeting by the door jamb. I had a few sweaty moments with the reptile book before I determined that it was a banded sand snake, noted for its ability to "swim in loose soil," and not a coral. The snake stuck its head out at various times that afternoon and was never seen again. A near-human screeching roused me one morning, and I stepped outside in time to watch a Gila woodpecker evict a starling from its hole in a saguaro. Shortly thereafter, on a bedroom curtain, I saw the largest hairless spider I have stared at without fear. These incursions, rather than frightening, were reassuring. The fallen saguaro even handed me a gift. Between its arms, spiders had suspended a mist net stuck with creosote leaves, giving the illusion that the limbs were fingers of land rising from scummy water. I was able to lift a cactus boot from one of these fingers; it was like snapping off a flower, a pomegranate flower in leather, round as a water drop, with a turned-back serrated lip.

Not until two-and-a-half years later, when I reread Willa Cather's *The Professor's House*, did I find some parallel to that four-month limbo. The last chapter of "Tom Outland's Story," her novella within a novel, finds protagonist Tom back on the Blue Mesa, in southwest Colorado, where he and a friend had discovered the cliff dwellings of a vanished civilization. Tom has returned from Washington, D.C., where he failed to interest the federal government in protecting the native heritage at Blue Mesa. Ashamed of his defeat, he finds that the friend, in his absence, has sold the artifacts they found together. The friend actually felt he was acting in Tom's behalf—raising the money to put Tom through college—but Tom accuses him of selling "what belonged to you and me, boys that have no other ancestors to inherit from," and drives his friend away, never to find him again. Realizing too late his own part in destroying a friendship that had been at the core of his emotional life, seeing the first defilement of a civilization that had been preserved intact for centuries, Tom remains on Blue Mesa for the summer. One would expect a season of grief amid this double ruin, but Tom finds, to paraphrase Cather, that for the first time the mesa comes together as a whole in his understanding, that he is simplified into a great happiness: that instead of losing everything, he has found everything. In his most self-damning moment, Tom calls himself "frightened at my own heartlessness."

While I had always considered "Tom Outland's Story" the single greatest fiction about the American West, its last chapter had put me off. How could Cather's appealing character, in the face of human betrayal and natural despoliation, experience such exaltation? Then I reread it two-and-a-half years after my own mother's death in a shock of self-recognition. A battered five-acre spread within the smog zone of Phoenix was scarcely Tom's Blue Mesa, nor could my dealings with bankers, lawyers, realtors, heirs of Frank, and friends of my mother compare with his solitude. My mother's relatively quick, clean passing, after harmonious seasons, spared me the estrangement of Tom's broken friendship. Yet I felt on the property—sure to be further blighted just as Mesa Verde, on which Cather's Blue Mesa was based, was to become an overburdened national park—a fullness, a strange rootedness without attachments. I watched, alert but passive, letting the outside invade the interior, glad for the snake under the carpet. I even leveled at myself, unaware I was soon to reread it in Cather, the word "heartless." How had Cather known this unreasonable truth, and what truth was it? Was it the sureness of something coming to an end, allowing you to embrace it without restraint? Inadequate, that is as close as I can come.

But the four-month idyll "to wind things up" had stored a climatic fright. I had invited Tom—not Cather's fiction but my own best friend in Phoenix—along with his wife, eight-year-old son, and son's friend, to what I had naively billed as a house-cooling party, at which they could select items they wanted before an estate sale to be held after I left. Because of an unseasonably hot winter, there had been grass fires already that spring, and I wasn't surprised when one of the boys said you could see a fire in back. I thought of fetching binoculars, then went to look first. Binoculars were unnecessary, for the fire had reached the crisper and was advancing toward the house. I called to Tom's wife, who punched 911, while Tom strung hoses together and ran them to the field. After these years of drift, these suspended four months, was I to wind things up with a conflagration? The air was almost still, but a slight breeze blew crosswise to the house rather than toward it, and Tom had the flames checked by the time the fire department, with three engines and a dozen volunteers, arrived minutes later. Men and machines drenched the area until it stopped smoking, and the event was over as offhandedly as it began. "Now you can have a fire sale instead of an estate sale," remarked Tom, recoiling the hose. The fire had started in the classic manner: the eight-year-olds had been experimenting with matches from the house, had tried to stamp out their success, and had run then to the house yelling that flames had erupted out of nowhere. Damage to property amounted to some charred fencing. The fire trucks entered where our neighbor had hauled out his citrus clippings, mashing the small barrier I had erected and compacting most of the soil between our house and the next. Several supernovae of prickly pear had burnt to extinction and a half-acre of creosote and bursage lay reduced to ash.

I look back on the twelve years of my mother's occupancy of those acres and see that our intention to leave the desert alone resulted, unwittingly, in loss after loss, simply by our being there. The desert, equally unwittingly, had given and given in return: to my mother, a beautiful setting and occasional subject for painting; to me, companionship, anxiety, and four months of what I decided, at the time, was heartlessness. The day after the fire I lay behind the paloverdes as doves dipped placidly into the water, mockingbirds scattered the finches, and thrashers craned from the faucet to catch the drops whose inverted world was as coherent as the one I watched from. Nothing, as usual, had happened. In spite of a central loss for me and many losses for the desert, life went on with its business and looked the other way. While I had no thought for Willa Cather at the time, I did think of the last line of a poem I had by heart. "Comfort that does not comprehend," said Edna St. Vincent Millay of the teeming indifference that receives our griefs, giving us strength from dedication that passes us by. It is hard to imagine why such irrelevance helps.

It is simply invigorating to be surrounded by creatures that drink and squawk and reroot and decline to care.

Ultimately there was no way I could help caring, and I only regretted all that escaped notice in the five compromised acres I explored as best I could. In the future I would prefer to be comforted by deserts that are wilder, less abused by myself, and if speech is necessary, perhaps instead of English it could be Spanish, a language raucous as the desert birds. But because this frayed remnant saw me through so much, it will keep replenishing itself through some crack in my attention, nourishing the next people who plant themselves, willfully, in its heart.

About the Author

BRUCE BERGER is the author of *The Telling Distance: Conversations with the American Desert*, first published in 1990, which won the 1990 Western States Book Award for Nonfiction and the 1991 Colorado Book Authors Award for Nonfiction. His earlier books include *Notes of a Half-Aspenite*, *A Dazzle of Hummingbirds*, and *Hangin' On*. His poetry has been published in periodicals such as *New Letters*, *Poetry*, *Barron's*, *Westways*, and *Commonweal*. He holds a B.A. in English from Yale University and has played the piano professionally in the United States and Spain. He currently lives in Aspen, Colorado, and spends part of the year in La Paz, Baja California Sur, Mexico, where he is helping in the Mexican government's program to rescue the endangered Peninsular pronghorn. He also is writing a book on Baja California.